Ship Modeling

S I M P L I F I E D

Ship Modeling

S I M P L I F I E D

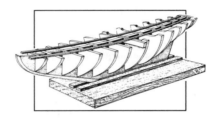

*Tips and Techniques
for Model Construction from Kits*

Frank Mastini

International Marine
Camden, Maine

International Marine/
Ragged Mountain Press
A Division of The McGraw-Hill Companies

24 25

Library of Congress Cataloging -in-Publication Data

Mastini, Frank.
    Ship modeling simplified: tips and techniques for model building from kits /
Frank Mastini
        p.   cm.
     ISBN 0-07-155867-5
     1. Ship models—Amateurs' manuals.   I. Title.
   VM298.M355   1990
   623.8'201—dc20   89-71640
                                                  CIP

Questions regarding the content of this book should be addressed to:

International Marine
P. O. Box 220
Camden, Maine 04843

Questions regarding the ordering of this book should be addressed to:

The McGraw -Hill Companies
Customer Service Department
P.O. Box 547
Blacklick, OH 43004
Retail Customers: 1-800-262-4729
Bookstores: 1-800-722-4726

Dedication

To my wife Lucy for her countless hours of support: Without her help this book never would have been completed. And to the memory of Barney Rehder, my teacher, my inspiration, and my dear friend.

CONTENTS

Introduction

I've written this book to bring the time-honored craft of building model ships to people who have been smitten — but perhaps intimidated — by the idea of building, say, a fully rigged 18th century man o'war. This book's simple methods were honed by my 25 years at the workbench, and by years of helping new modelers grapple with their first projects. These methods will make it possible for an inexperienced person to build a model of which he can be proud.

Back in the 1800s Darcy Lever wrote in his bountifully illustrated guide for novice British midshipmen, *The Young Sea Officer's Sheet Anchor*, "A mere verbal explanation often perplexes the mind, for no one but a seaman can clearly comprehend it; and he is not the object for whom such aid is intended." Mr. Lever's thoughts, though almost 200 years old, are still applicable. In this book you'll find an abundance of illustrations to help you along.

A ship model is the product of a builder's efforts and perseverance. It will take you many demanding hours to finish a model. During this time you'll be washed with waves of conflicting emotions, rising and falling with each success or failure. All this will be a part of an experience that will be yours alone: Your first model may not be a showpiece, but I promise you from personal experience that it will be the one you never give away.

Your most important tool for success will be dedication, which, according to the *American Heritage Dictionary of the English Language*, is committing "one's self to a particular course of thought or action." Add some enthusiasm and a positive mental attitude, and you'll have a formidable edge when you sit down to tackle your first model.

You'll make mistakes, sometimes big ones; at times you'll be confused. You must believe that you can overcome these setbacks, correct them, and move on. This book will be there with advice and encouragement when you need it.

We'll move step by step through the often bewildering array of alternatives that an aspiring modeler faces. You'll find instructions on tools — from the simplest to the most complicated — and how to use them. You'll learn the best way to set up a workshop, what to look for in kits, and what to expect when you open them. I'll take you through the logical steps of building a complicated ship model, helping you avoid the pitfalls that trap most beginners.

You'll also find a dictionary of technical nautical terms translated from Italian to English that will allow you to understand the instructions and legends in Italian-made kits, which are marketed in abundance. A glossary of nautical terms defines every part of a ship's anatomy.

All the information you need is right here; now it's up to you to choose the right model. Just remember this: The hours you'll spend building the model will be scant compared with the hours you'll spend showing it off. The pride you'll gain will more than overshadow the frustrations and struggles of building it. The skills you pick up along the way will be yours forever and will boost your confidence when you start your next model.

A ship model should be enjoyed by every member of your family. If you're married, make your wife or husband part of your plans and dreams — possibly a partner. If you have children, allow them to participate in some aspect of your new hobby. Making it a family hobby promotes togetherness and keeps the art of ship model building alive for another generation. Life goes on — so why not ship model building too?

Let me prove that you too can build a beautiful ship model.

— Frank Mastini

Ship Modeling

SIMPLIFIED

PART I
Setting Up Shop

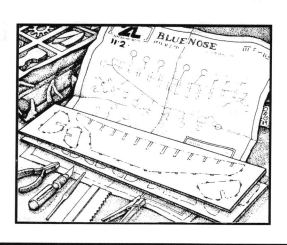

SELECTING A KIT

Take a look at the models on display at your local hobby shop. Manufacturers worldwide have produced a huge variety of kits, and that's a good sign. You'll have no shortage of new projects to take on as you gain experience. But where do you start?

An enthusiastic beginner looking for his first model is confronted with a fascinating, but very confusing, array of choices. Although all kits provide certain basic materials, there are significant differences in type and quality. Here are some things to keep in mind when making a selection.

MAKING YOUR CHOICE

Choose a model that catches your eye, but heed the limits facing a first-timer.

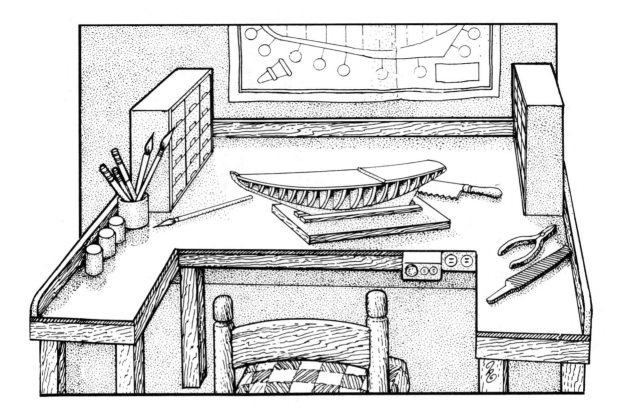

Your decision will have a lot to do with the mood you are in and the pleasure you get from thinking about how the finished model will look. Realistically, though, as when choosing a new car, you should consider several factors before making the final decision. How much money do you want to spend? How much experience do you have? What kind of display space will be available for the finished model? What kind of ship attracts you? Are the kits that interest you

of good quality? How much time can you spend at the workbench?

Sound too involved? Well, it's not if you're sensible. Think "simple" for your first effort. Though you're looking for a challenge, you're not looking for intense frustration.

Your Ability

I have known many novices to buy kits of the magnitude of the *Sovereign of the*

Seas, *San Felipe*, or *Amerigo Vespucci*—ships with multiple decks, intricate ornamentation, and complicated rigging plans. They bought them, but they never finished them. What I saw instead was frustration, failure, and dejection — and, of course, the abandonment of what could have been a happy and successful pastime.

Choose a fairly small, simple, attractive but complete model, one that has a bit of everything found in ships. Look for a model with one deck, one or two masts and simple rigging. A good example would be a Baltimore Clipper from around the time of the War of 1812, or a fishing schooner such as *Bluenose II*. Such a vessel will introduce the first-timer to the art of building the hull (especially the plank-on-bulkhead type). You'll plank decks and build deck fixtures (gratings, pumps, binnacles, fife rails and pin rails, winches, capstans, ladders). If you choose a Baltimore Clipper you'll learn how to cut gunports and how to assemble and rig guns in place. You'll move on to building and rigging simple spars and masts. Such a model, in other words, will be sufficiently complex to teach you many basic skills, but not so much so that you never receive the satisfaction of successfully completing it.

Some good kits that are simple enough for beginners include *Lynx*, *Gladis*, and *Dallas* by Pan Art; *Bluenose II*, *Harvey*, and *Mare Nostrum* by Artesania Latina; *Flying Fish* by Corel; *America* by Mamoli; and *Dandy II* by Dikar.

PHOTO 1. *A beginner's nightmare. The stern ornamentation, the sheer of the hull, and the multiple gun decks of the* San Felipe *spell disaster for a first-time builder.*

THE COST

It's always a good idea to shop around before actually purchasing a kit: There's a wide range of prices out there reflecting quality, size, and production costs. Prices vary from manufacturer to manufacturer for the same ship. For instance, four or five manufacturers offer kits of the *Constitution* at four or five different prices. Throw in the vast differences among hobby retailers and you can see the need for comparison shopping.

My advice for a modeler looking for his first project: Don't spend more than $150.

When you get to the hobby shop, bring with you all these considerations

PHOTO 2. *The simple hull line and rigging plan of the schooner* Bluenose II *allow a beginner to learn and refine basic planking and rigging skills. The exposed section shows the first layer of planking.*

as well as your checkbook or charge card. Leave some of your enthusiasm at home where it will be waiting for you when you arrive with your purchase. A cool, knowledgeable shopper who knows what he wants is the most likely to get it.

SCALE

Kits come in a number of scales — a way of comparing the size of the model with the size of the real ship. Scale will become more important as you refine your modeling skills. For now it's not something to worry a great deal about. Stick to the types of models I've recommended and go with whatever scale the manufacturer has decided to use.

Still, it's important to understand what scale is. Scale is expressed as a ratio: maybe 1/50 or 1:25 or 1/96. What does that mean?

Say we're talking about a model in which 1/4 inch represents one foot on the full-size ship. The scale might be called a 1/4-inch scale or, more likely, a 1:48 scale (1 foot — that's 12 inches — divided by 1/4 inch equals 48); they're both the same. In 1:48 scale the 143-foot *Bluenose II* would be 35 1/2 inches long.

But there are other scales — and the

matter is complicated further by European kits, which use ratios expressed in metric dimensions. Let's save ourselves some headaches and compare three common scales.

- A 1:96 scale is similar to a 1/8-inch American scale: one foot on the full-size ship is represented by 1/8 inch or about 3 mm. (A three-foot-high bulwark on the full-size ship would be 3/8 inch or 9 mm on your model.)
- A 1:75 metric scale is similar though not equivalent to a 3/16-inch American scale: one foot on the full-size ship is represented by 3/16 inch or 4.5 mm. (A three-foot high bulwark on the full-size ship would be 9/16 inch or 13.5 mm on your model.)
- A 1:48 scale is equivalent to a 1/4-inch American scale: one foot on the full-size ship is represented by 1/4 inch or about 6 mm. (A three-foot-high bulwark on the full-size ship would be 3/4 inch or 18 mm on your model.)

Don't think in abstract terms; apply the scales to real-life situations and your experience will be painless.

METRIC VS. INCHES. This brings up another mildly troublesome problem. When you're working with a European kit do you try to convert everything to inches? If you want to make extra work for yourself go ahead. If you've purchased a European kit, think metric; if

PHOTO 3. *Universal ruler. The metric and the inch scales face each other in the center— no calculations necessary.*

you have an American kit, think inches and feet.

Sometimes you *will* need to convert a measurement from inches to metric or vice versa — and that takes time. I have a way around that problem, a little gadget I call my universal ruler. Go to an art supply store and find two rulers, one in inches and the other in metric — preferably one with a righthand scale and one with a lefthand scale.

If you can't find a righthand ruler, cover the numbers on one ruler with masking tape and re-write them from right to left. With the metric and inch scales facing each other, glue the two rulers to a wooden base. Instant conversion.

WHAT TO LOOK FOR IN A MODEL

You don't have to be an expert to choose a good kit. All you have to do is look at the quality of the contents thoroughly.

You have a right to do so, and if you can't look inside the box, don't buy the kit.

That, of course, can lead to problems if you're buying from a catalog. The best way to avoid unpleasant surprises is sticking to manufacturers and suppliers whose reputations are solid. Ordering kits from some manufacturers virtually guarantees you'll get what you want. Some mail order suppliers will replace broken or missing parts. Call before ordering and find out what the supplier's policy is. On the other hand, some hobby shops will have nothing to do with you after your purchase. Ask around, and be circumspect.

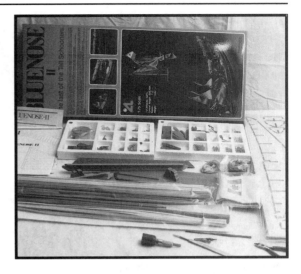

PHOTO 4. *The kit of the* Bluenose II *by Artesania Latina, a Spanish manufacturer. The number of pieces can be staggering, even for a simple model; check to make sure everything listed is there, and in good condition.*

THE PLANS

The plans include all the drawings you need to assemble the model. The degree of precision and the quality of the drawings generally will spell victory or defeat for a beginner. To take full advantage of any set of plans, however, you should be familiar with overall construction principles, including the anatomy of rigging, or you'll be lost. In fact, I'd strongly suggest reading through this entire book to get an idea of what kinds of things to look for before you commit yourself to a selection.

Generally, you'll find that every manufacturer uses its own system, with different geometrical or three-dimensional drawings. Some include black and white pictures of the different parts or stages of construction; some use coded letters with legends to describe parts and rigging lines. The best ones use an exploded view of the model and mark different parts with numbers that guide you to detailed drawings of that particular piece or setting.

INSTRUCTIONS

If the instructions accompanying the plans are not explicit you could be in trouble before you start. Check the instructions to see how clearly they are written. On some kits, the step-by-step methods are actually out of sequence.

Some of the plans carry instructions written in a foreign language (Italian, for the most part), and because the terms are nautical and technical, you can't translate them with a standard dictionary. (You'll find a translation of those terms from Italian to English beginning on page 115.) Some methods lead to confusion because they will contrast unnecessarily with the methods used in other kits.

The Hull

Disregarding plastic, there are three types of hulls found in model kits: solid hulls; plank-on-frame (or plank-on-bulkhead); or precut plywood on frames. You'll learn the distinction between frames and bulkheads in Part II.

The solid hull can provide an easy step for beginners, because it needs only minor shaping and sanding to finish. Solid hulls are machine shaped, which often creates bulwarks — the parapets around the outside of the deck — that are much too thick. To correct this you must reduce the bulwarks with a chisel, rasp, or sandpaper. This is quite a challenge for beginners because you stand a good chance of splitting the wood and ruining the job. Let me put it this way: If you build a model with a solid hull you miss all the experience and fun of planking. The same thing applies to precut plywood. Plank-on-frame gives the builder a feeling for how a real ship was built. The other two hull types don't.

Wooden Parts

Kits are *supposed* to supply all the wooden parts you need to complete your model. In truth, unfortunately, you'll find it hard to finish your model with what you find in the box. Some parts will be badly cut and cannot be used; some are distorted, some are too short. A careful shopper will check this out before he forks over his money. Some stores will let you check, others won't. As with catalogs, find out what a store's policy is on replacing parts. The first thing you should do when you get home is get out the kit's checklist and make sure every strip of wood is there and in good shape.

Here's an example: Most kits supply the dowels needed to build your spars. The problem is figuring out how to cut the correct pieces from a certain dowel length. Most of the time you'll end up with pieces that are too short and can't be used for all the parts needed. But you can always buy extra dowels.

Often, scribed decks are supplied with kits. They may be nice looking but are far from authentic. If measured in scale, some of the planks would be hundreds of feet long. You can always scribe more plank ends, but the best thing to do in this case is to plank the deck yourself, as I'll explain later.

Some precut decks are made of plywood that's much too thin to stand up on its own. When nailed and glued to the frame it sags and buckles atrociously.

PHOTO 5. *Most kits supply the dowels you'll need to build your masts and yards, but you'll have to cut them to their correct lengths.*

PHOTO 6. *Properly turned out deck fixtures — railing stanchions, cleats, gratings, gun barrels and the like — can add a great deal to your model's appearance.*

I'll show you ways to correct this problem.

Take great care in removing precut parts from their sheets. These parts are precut on one side only; if you attempt to remove them without first cutting through them with a knife, they will break up or tear along their edges.

THE FITTINGS

Fittings — such as blocks, railing stanchions, gun carriages, gun barrels, doors, chains, cleats, pumps, and gratings — are an essential element to the beauty of a model. Some kits have metal fittings, some have plastic, some wood. Look inside the box before you buy, for the quality of the fittings should help guide your selection and may even decide the issue.

Brass fittings are by far the most attractive and easiest to work with. Fittings made from britannia, a silver-white alloy similar to pewter, can be quite handsome.

Consider also the amount of finish work these fittings will require. Some fittings will have to be cleaned of casting excesses. Some will have to be redrilled because the holes in them are almost nonexistent. The precut pieces needed to make the gratings are sometimes roughly cut, and can be quite a challenge to clean out. You can check such things without opening the plastic

PHOTO 7. *Even the simplest kits for the serious beginner provide a wealth of intricate fixtures you can assemble and embellish, such as this schooner's wheel, fife rail, house, pump, and windlass.*

PHOTO 8. *. . . Or these lathe-turned barrels and capstan.*

PHOTO 9. *. . . Or this aft latrine from the schooner* Harvey; *note the doorknob.*

PHOTO 10. *This bilge pump and forward rail from the* Harvey *are part of the kit; all you need is a steady hand.*

PHOTO 11. *Other fixtures you may find in your kit will add flavor, such as this workbench . . .*

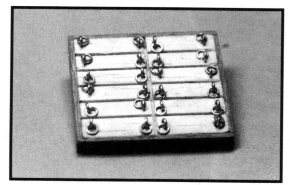

PHOTO 12. *. . . Or this main hatch, complete with metal fittings . . .*

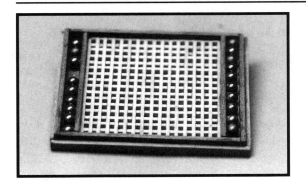

PHOTO 13. . . . *Or this grating cover and cannonball rack.*

box or bag in which the fittings are stored.

THE BOATS

Lifeboats, whale boats, service boats — most kits include them. They may be metal, plastic, precarved wood, or precut plank on frame. Here again every type has its merits or faults; the important criterion is quality.

The precast boats can be quite authentic-looking and handsome. Although undeniably beautiful, the precut plank-on-frame boats can pose quite a challenge for the builder; they are to me, however, the most authentic and the most satisfying. A built-up whale boat is a pretty thing to see, though it also represents hours of challenging work. It doesn't matter if you fail; you can always try again or buy a precarved one.

If the boats are not supplied with the kit, always make or buy the right ones

for the model you are building. How? Go to a library and check any number of historical references. Try, for example, *The History of American Sailing Ships*, or *The American Fishing Schooners* by Howard I. Chapelle.

Boats should be equipped with oars, harpoons, and other such accessories as appropriate. You can buy oars from hobby shops or catalogs, or you can make them yourself — and that is definitely the most fun. Some kits will show ways of doing it.

RIGGING LINES

It's distressing to have to say that 90 percent of the kits on the market today fall short in supplying acceptable rigging lines and cables. Most include rigging of the wrong size or color.

PHOTO 14. *A ship's boat lashed to the foredeck, a touch of authenticity, and a challenge to build.*

PHOTO 15. *Shrouds, stays, ratlines, and lifts — a cat's cradle of rigging that can quickly get out of control if you don't pay attention to scale.*

BUILDING A WORKPLACE

TOOLS: VALUABLE ASSETS

Tools are a craftsman's best friend: The quality of your tools will determine the quality of your finished product. Tools improve your ability, save time and effort, and preserve your attitude. There is nothing more frustrating than working with the wrong tools or with tools that are in bad condition.

I've broken down the tools you'll need into three categories: basic, intermediate, and expert. In addition, I've developed some tools and laborsaving arrangements you can make yourself.

BASIC TOOLS. The following hand tools are essential to build any model. Building without them would be like trying to build a house without a saw. A set of the following essential tools will probably run you about $100. Shop around; the best place to buy this type of equipment is a hobby shop, where you have a chance to see first-hand what you're buying. Here's what you'll need:

Some kits supply white string so thick your finished model will look like a Christmas tree. Only a very few kits provide acceptable rigging line. Check to see what comes with the one you're thinking of buying. The best type is three-strand twisted linen. Black is the most useful color for standing rigging; you'll need other colors — gray, beige (cream), and brown — for other jobs aboard your model. Twisted cotton line is also available. It is practically impossible to find rigging line correct for models of 1/8-inch (1/96) scale or smaller, but with a little persistence you can come pretty close. You can find rigging line as small as 0.10 mm in diameter.

- Pliers: Longnose (needlenose), roundtip, sidecutter, and flattip; pliers should be no more than 5 inches long and should have plastic-covered handles for a better grip.
- Hammers: One small carpenter type and one ball peen.

PHOTO 16. *Without these basic tools, it's tough to get going: Pliers, cutting blades, clips, a compass, straightedges, files, and brushes — even a clothespin.*

- Saws: A razor-type X-Acto with handle, and miter box (aluminum type, if possible); a good coping saw with a fine-tooth blade; a hole-cutting X-Acto blade with handle. Some stores sell combinations of these tools in sets; the X-Acto saw handles are interchangeable.
- Chisels: A small set of carving chisels; X-Acto type chisel blade with handle.
- Knives: A set of X-Acto knives; surgeon's scalpel with #11 blade.
- Files: A set of small files, including a medium bastard, a fine round, a fine flat, and a fine half-round.
- Drills: Pin-vise type hand drill; one set of drill bits from #60 to #80; one set of drill bits from 1/32 inch to 1/4 inch.

- Electric plank bender: A must for perfection and ease in plank bending, plank installation, and other uses. (It will cost around $25; if you don't want to spend the money yet, an electric hair-curling iron will work, but not nearly as well.)
- Rasps: One flat and one half-round carpenter's rasp.
- Needle threaders: One package.
- Tweezers.
- Rulers: Yardstick; 12-inch plastic and steel rulers and metric equivalents.
- Squares: One small and one large plastic.
- Compass: Regular classroom type.
- Awl: No thicker than 1/16 inch.
- Clamps: One dozen alligator-type clips; one package of clip-type

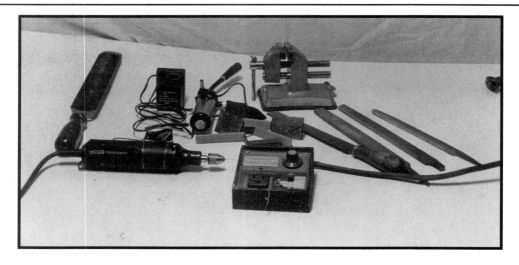

PHOTO 17. *An electric drill with a speed reducer, a mini-vise with a "suction-cup" bottom, and a mini-vacuum cleaner can help move things along quickly, and cleanly.*

clothespins; a set of three different sizes (one-, two-, and three-inch) of steel clamps.

- Sanding blocks: A chalkboard eraser; some small wood blocks, triangular and square — with flat and rounded surfaces.
- Sandpaper: Aluminum oxide is best: rough, medium, and fine (#80, #120, #320).
- Brushes: One set each of nylon and sable flat brushes, sizes 1 to 4.
- Plane: A small hobby plane.
- Scissors: At least one pair of regular dressmaking shears; one pair smaller embroidery/craft scissors.
- Vise: Vacuum-base type that can be moved easily on the bench.
- Glue: Carpenter's glue and cyano-acrylate glue (ACC). I like a brand called Super Jet, but there are a number of others.
- Pins: A number of sizes; a must for planking and for temporary clamping.

INTERMEDIATE TOOLS. You might want to try a few models before investing in these tools, but they will help you do a better job in a shorter time. They also represent a substantial investment. Remember, shop around.

- Drill (motorized tool): Electric, with a complete set of carving and cutting tools; the drill should have a universal chuck, not a collet — a speed-reducing transformer is a must. (Try the Maxicraft set with the various attachments.) Around $110.

- Soldering iron: Pistol-grip type with two heat levels. Around $25.
- Miter box: Adjustable to angles from 0 to 90 degrees. Around $15.
- Rasps: A set of rasps with offset handles for better handling, including flat, concave, round, and triangular shapes; also get a plane-type rasp with a replaceable blade. Around $15.
- Turntable: This homemade base will help in rigging your model; adapt a lazy susan-type base by installing a shelving or plywood board on top of it. By setting your model on this base, you'll be able to turn it around easily when working on the deck or when rigging. Around $5.
- Waterline marker: We'll learn how to make one on page 54.
- Cutting jig for deck planks: See page 41.
- Mast setting jig: See page 98.
- Universal vise: This type will permit you to adjust the angle of the jaws in many positions. Around $25.
- Magnifying glass: Will help for close-up work. Around $15.
- 1/4-inch variable speed electric drill. Around $35.
- Electric drill stand. Around $10.

TOOLS FOR THE EXPERT. Here are some tools to think about when you're sure you've caught the ship modeling bug.

A FEW WORDS OF ADVICE ON TOOLS

- Cheap tools don't last and don't work.
- Each tool should have its own storage spot. You'll get to it quickly and be able to tell at a glance what's missing.
- Use your tools as they were intended—a screwdriver is not a chisel, a plastic ruler is not a cutting guide.
- Keep your tools clean and sharp. A dull X-Acto doesn't cut, and it could be dangerous.
- Hard surfaces wreak havoc on fine-bladed tools; try to keep them apart.
- Unplug all electrical tools when finished.
- Store spare saw blades in cardboard covers; you'll protect the blades and your fingers.
- Don't use your electric saw on wood that makes it strain. Sharpen the saw's blades.
- Keep your power table clear of sawdust; fire isn't funny.
- Use protective glasses when working with power tools.
- Clean your paint brushes immediately with thinners and then soap and water; they'll last longer.

They cost a bit and require refined skills, so don't rush out to buy them until you're confident in your growing competence. We won't concern ourselves with prices here; just consider this equipment to dream about.

- 7-1/2-inch electric table saw: This type of saw should be at least 3/4 horsepower. To ensure a true cut, the rip guide should be built so that it can be secured accurately on both ends. The best rip guides are those that slide with a bushing on a solid shaft at both ends. The saw should be adjustable to tilt at various angles.
- 4-inch electric table saw: This saw is used for very close, accurate, and clean work, using a jeweler's blade for a smooth finish. Here again be aware of the construction of the rip guide and the motor's horsepower (at least 3/4 hp). Check the blade slot in the saw table. If it is too wide your fine strips will be drawn under while you're cutting them; a problem you can remedy by using a piece of scrap plywood 3 mm to 5 mm (1/8 to 3/16 inch) thick. Set the piece on the table and cut it about halfway through the blade, then run your strip on top of it while cutting it. The scrapwood base will prevent your strip from being drawn through the table slot.
- Electric scroll saw: A band-type scroll used for making curved cuts; a vibrating scroll saw (buy one with a clearance of at least 16 inches).
- Bench grinder: A small one will do the job.
- Bench sanders: 1-inch belt sander (good for small parts precision sanding); a 4-inch belt sander (possibly with a disc sanding attachment and a table with an adjustable guide).
- Lathe: Bench type, preferably with speed control. The lathe bed must be at least 18 inches long.
- Mini-vac: This miniature vacuum cleaner will help remove dust and small particles from very hard-to-get-at places.

GETTING SET TO BUILD

WORKBENCH. Depending on the space available, your workbench should be large enough to allow you to work on any size model, plus hold the tools you use constantly. A strong, good-sized bench could be made from a 4- by 6-foot sheet of 3/4-inch plywood. Take a look at Figure 2. Two side extensions approximately 1 foot by 2 feet provide extra accessibility to parts and tools as you work. The bench should be about 32 inches high; place a small cabinet with plastic drawers for spare parts on each end of the bench. You can also store small tools, such as drill bits and knife blades, in those drawers. On the front right side of the bench (left, if you're lefthanded) attach your transformer for your motorized tool (which you may not

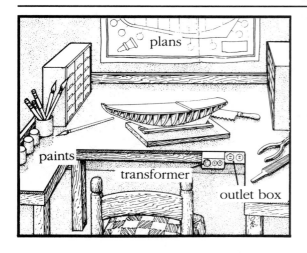

FIGURE 2. *A neat workbench, with everything in reach, can make a modeler's task infinitely easier. Note how the plans are pinned behind the bench to save space and ease reading.*

buy at first, but probably will eventually if you keep at modeling) and some electrical outlets. Don't take up workspace with the plans. Rather, hang them on the wall directly in front of you and all around the bench, so that you can consult them without getting off your chair.

POWER TABLE. Use one table to hold all your power machines. It should be at least 4 by 6 feet, preferably made from 3/4-inch plywood. Arrange your machines as illustrated (Figure 3); believe me, it will cut down on interference and strain. Install a multi-outlet box in the middle of the bench to avoid creating a maze of electrical cords. No wood scraps,

parts, or tools should ever be left on the power table.

THE MASTINI BOOSTER. Working on a delicate rigging problem or cutting a planking section takes the steady hands of a surgeon. The close-range work of ship model building is tough enough without adding to the strain on your arms, lower back, and shoulder and neck muscles because your work chair is too high or too low. And lifting your arms without support makes them unsteady. My solution: the Mastini Booster.

I use an ordinary captain's chair with a padded seat fitted across the arm rests. I sit on the elevated seat with my feet on the original seat. My elbows rest on my knees, supporting my back and steadying my hands. The back and neck pains are gone. This arrangement also allows me to rest a wooden board on my knees for closer work when necessary.

Find a chair that won't be insulted by paint stains and sawdust, push it up to your workbench, then craft a way to allow you to work with your hands at rest on your legs. Rather than straining to reach up to work, your hands are relaxed and free — and at table level. You can work for hours without strain. It's the only way to go. (See Figure 4.)

UTILITY TABLES. These tables will come in handy for your kit box, other parts you want out of the way, measuring tools, and some of the plan sheets,

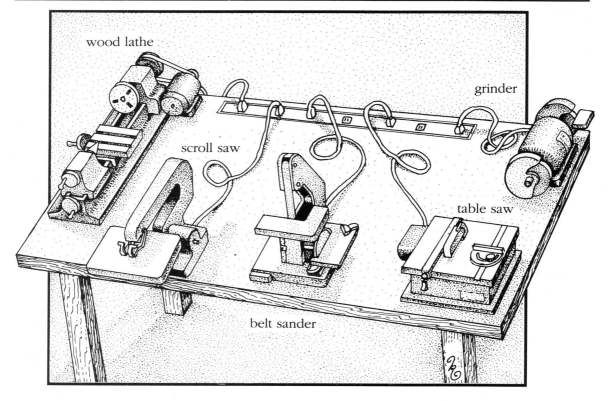

FIGURE 3. *Set up a power table adjacent to your main workbench. Arrange your appliances to prevent crossed wires and awkward reaches. Most beginners won't need this much heavy artillery.*

etc. You may also use them as display platforms for taking photographs.

LIGHTING. Good lighting is extremely important for the quality of your work and, of course, to protect your eyes. Use a two-bulb, 40-watt fluorescent light arrangement above each of your tables and the workbench. In addition, install one bright spotlight on a swivel above your workbench to direct light where it

is needed. Don't use bench-mounted extension lights because they will get in the way of your model. For safety reasons, no extension cords should be hanging over or near your bench.

VENTILATION. Good ventilation is a prime concern when working with fumes from varnishes, paints, glues, and solvents. It will also dissipate excess heat from lights. If your workplace sits apart

FIGURE 4. *The Mastini Booster.*

from any windows, install a small bathroom-type exhaust fan above your bench and connected to a dryer hose vented to the outside.

SLOP SINK. It's also extremely important to have a slop sink nearby. You don't want to walk a mile to wash your brushes, fill your jar, or get a few drops of water to dilute your glue. Unless you live alone — or would like to shortly — avoid using the kitchen sink.

SHELVES. The more shelves you can install on the walls of your work area, the easier your life will be. Unlike boxes, shelves display their contents at a glance, saving time and temper. Masonite perforated board (pegboard) with removable hooks also is a lifesaver.

PART II

Building the Hull

"The Topmast Studding Sail is bent to a Yard, with Knittles and Earings, and frequently laced to it. This Sail has sometimes a Reefband in it. It is gored in the outer Leech, according to the Length of the Boom, and the Squareness of the Yard, and also at the Head from the outer to the inner Earing."

—The Young Sea Officer's Sheet Anchor, *1819*

The language of the sea has a life of its own, developed over hundreds of years. Someone just learning English and a Ph.D who's studied the language for 30 years are on an equal footing when they begin their first models. At times it can be intimidating: Just what the heck are the instructions talking about?

Before we start assembling our first model, here are some simple things to visualize. We start with the *keel*, the ship's main structural member. The keel runs longitudinally down the ship's centerline, from *stem* (or *bow*) — the front — to *stern* — the rear. Everything is built up and out from the keel.

Next we add other pieces at right angles to the centerline formed by the keel. These pieces will run *athwartships* and will add strength and stability to the hull. These are *bulkheads*, the bases of which you're going to attach to the keel. For the purposes of this book we'll call them *bulkhead frames*. (On a

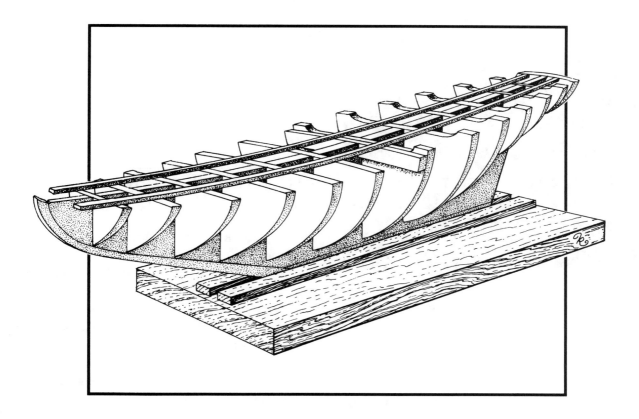

real ship, frames are rib-like girders that run athwartships from the keel to the deckline. They stabilize the hull and provide shape and a base for planking.)

If you can picture this simple assembly, you'll have no problem as we move into our construction phase.

The trick to assembling plank-on-bulkhead models is patience. You'll be assembling a lot of often rough-cut wooden pieces — frames, keel sections, decks — into what is supposed to be a very precise, symmetrical hull. One piece out of kilter can throw the entire model off. And then you can throw the entire model out.

On your first run-through everything should be assembled, piece by delicate piece, without going near the glue. I have developed several methods that will teach you how to check symmetry, and how to make sure that when you're finally ready to assemble everything, it will fit.

PHOTO 18. *Real-life construction techniques may vary from those of models, but once the hull is planked and decked the result looks the same.*

Keep your hands off the glue until we're ready. I'll give you a nudge now and then while we're checking things to make sure you don't just say: "Well, it looks good to me, let's glue it."

Don't.

In building any ship model it's essential that the work follow a known, logical pattern. Otherwise it's all too easy to feel overwhelmed. And it's all that much harder for beginners, who have not yet developed a sense of procedure and may make things much harder than they have to.

Read through the following steps to get an idea of how we'll proceed. The approach I've outlined here has proven its effectiveness over the years. The details for each step of the process are covered more thoroughly later as we make our way through the construction. Let's get started.

SEQUENCE FOR BUILDING THE HULL

Step 1: Check your kit. Open the kit box and look through the contents; get an idea of what each part looks like. Almost every kit contains an instruction booklet with a checklist of all the parts. Make sure that all the parts are there, that the wood strips are intact, and that all the plastic envelopes holding small, loose parts are sealed. Also, check to make sure that *all* the plans are in the kit. If they're not, call your mail order house or retailer immediately.

Step 2: Assemble the keel. Remove the keel parts. (Some kits have a one-piece keel, others may have more than one piece.) Take the assembly drawing and tack or hang it up over your workbench. That way you'll be able to see it easily while you're assembling the framework.

Step 3: Fit the frames to the keel. Check again that the frames are not broken or distorted and mark them for symmetry. File all the inserting cuts in the frames until they fit hand-tight in the keel.

Do not glue the frames on the keel until the assembly is completed.

Step 4: Check and fit the decks. This operation is extremely important because the decks will straighten the keel and help align the frames. Decks in kits are generally made in two different patterns. The false decks (like a subfloor in a house) used on models of single-deck ships such as schooners are generally made all in one piece and have no grooves to fit on the frame's bulwark extensions; while the decks used on multiple-deck ships do have precut grooves along both sides to fit around the bulwark extensions. Both these types must be centered on the keel and aligned with the frames. Never force the deck into place around the frames; that will buckle the decks and distort the hull.

Step 5: Put in wood blocks for masts. The method of installing masts varies with the manufacturer and the model. On some, wooden blocks are installed below the deck to provide a solid support for the masts. Other plans will show how to insert the mast through holes in the deck to the keel. I prefer to install wooden blocks on all models because it provides a more stable mast footing.

Step 6: Tack in the deck. Once you've fitted the decks, tack them in place *without gluing* using the pins supplied in the kit. If you need extra pins, sequin pins from a sewing shop are excellent; hobby shops will have them too. Make sure that the centering lines you have marked are aligned with the keel and the frames.

Step 7: Assemble and fit the bow and stern pieces. These solid wooden pieces will help give the proper shape to the model and provide a solid base for the ends of the planking. Pay careful attention to shaping these pieces; they must be symmetrical and follow the shape of the hull.

Step 8: Glue the frame assembly. After a final check to assure yourself that your framework is straight and your decks are not twisted or buckled, you can proceed to glue the framework. Let it dry at least 24 hours.

Step 9: Taper the frames. Once the glue is dry, you can begin to taper the front and back frames. Use a planking strip to check that the planking will sit flat against the bow and stern frames. File the frames until the strip rests flat against them.

Step 10: Install the gunport frames, if necessary.

Step 11: Plank the deck. If your model has no bulwark frame extensions, you can now plank the deck. If your model does have frame extensions, you will plank the deck when the hull planking has been completed and the extensions are removed (Step 15).

Step 12: Plank the hull. You can now begin the first layer of hull planking. When you plank the bulwark extensions be sure to install pieces of tape on the outside of the frames above the deck line so that the planks will not be glued to the extensions, which have to be removed later.

Step 13: Cut the gunports. If your model has posts that support dummy guns, you will have marked the position of these posts on the planks as you went along. If your model uses gunport frames, these will have already been installed before planking. This will enable you to locate the gunport's position correctly in front of the posts. When the first layer of planking is done, cut the gunports before sanding the hull so you don't erase your markings. When the second layer of planking is installed, you can cut the gunports as you plank over them. With other models, the gunports are cut into the completed planking.

Step 14: Install the second layer of hull planking, sand it smooth, and varnish.

Step 15: Plank the deck. If your model has bulwark frame extensions, remove them with an X-Acto saw blade and plank the deck. Varnish the deck.

Step 16: Plank and varnish the bulwarks.

Step 17: Install the wales, the channels, and the deadeyes.

Step 18: Put waterways and timberheads into place, if required.

Step 19: Paint, apply copper plating, and do ornamentation. If your model calls for the hull to be painted or coppered, you can do that now and then set your hull on its permanent base to avoid unwanted marks or scratches. If your model requires ornamentation of the bow and stern, finish that before installing the hull on its permanent base.

ASSEMBLING BULKHEAD-ON-KEEL HULLS

Very often the precut bulkheads — the solid athwartships pieces — found in plank-on-bulkhead ship models are out of symmetry and off center. If you assemble them without correcting the imperfections, you end up with an uneven hull profile. Figure 5 shows the method I use to check the frames.

Place a bulkhead frame from your kit on a sheet of thick paper (manila folders work best) and trace its outline **(1)**. Remove the bulkhead frame from the paper, and cut around the outline with a pair of scissors to create an exact paper pattern **(2)**. Next, fold the paper pattern **(3)**, making sure that the upper outer edges are matched and clipped or stapled together before you crease it in the middle. The crease will produce a true centerline and show if the lower outer edges are cut unevenly or if the keel slot in the frame is off center.

If the outer edges are misaligned, remove the excess on the pattern with scissors to even out the edges of the two halves. Return the folded pattern to the bulkhead frame **(4)**, mark and file off the excess on the frame itself, and draw the centerline (C). If the keel slot is out of center with the pattern, mark it on the bulkhead frame.

Now repeat this on the other side of the frame by just turning the pattern over and aligning it on the previously drawn centerline **(5)**. Next, correct the bulkhead frame's outer profile by filing off any excess you have marked. If the center slot is out of alignment with the centerline, glue on thin strips of wood to fill one side and remove the excess on the other side. Finally, draw the centerline on the top edge of the bulkhead. This mark will help line up the frame with the keel during the actual assembly. Repeat this procedure with every bulkhead and you'll have a symmetrical hull profile.

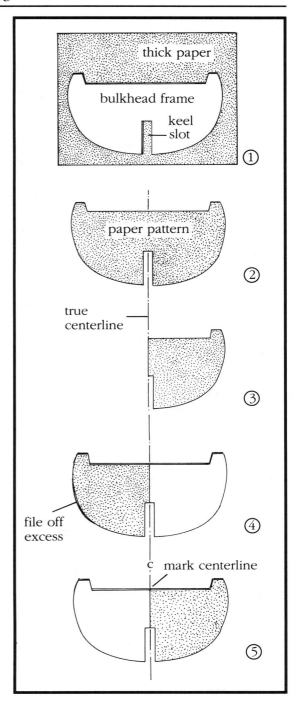

FIGURE 5. *Checking symmetry on bulkhead frames.*

Assembling the Keel

In the types of models I've suggested for beginners you'll be asked to assemble keels that come in two, three, or four sections. It is extremely important that you do this job as close to perfectly as possible to get a symmetrical, straight hull. Figure 6 shows how I attack this problem. Get a flat, straight piece of wood, such as a shelving board, and nail a 1-inch by 3/4-inch strip of wood along its length to form a baseboard on which the keel can be assembled. Each of the keel sections is notched where it keys to the next section forward or aft; these notches must be filed with *extreme* accuracy to allow the sections to fit smartly into one another. Make sure that the base of the keel is snug against the wooden baseboard for exact alignment.

Reinforce the joints with some small pieces cut from a sheet of 1/16-inch plywood. These pieces become a permanent part of the hull, so make sure they don't cover the bulkhead slots or extend below the keel on the bottom. To prevent the glued seams from sticking to the work surface, insert file cards between the keel and the board behind it. When everything is ready, glue and assemble the keel, applying pressure to the joints with clamps.

Aligning the Frames with the Keel

Here's another reminder: A very common mistake, and a very tempting one that I've seen a lot of people make, is to glue each bulkhead on the keel before checking the entire frame assembly. You've placed a bulkhead on the keel and it looks pretty good. Why not just glue it on?

Let me repeat: *Don't do it yet.* Doing so can lead to costly and frustrating delays. As the glue dries it will distort the frame, and the entire hull will be useless and have to be scrapped.

The proper method is first to assemble the entire frame, fastening the deck, the provided strengtheners, or both temporarily using small pins. Once you've checked the entire assembly for alignment and symmetry, glue it together and remove the pins.

Variations on Construction

False decks. Plank-on-bulkhead kits require a range of assembly methods, but

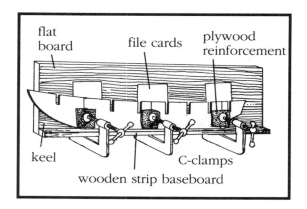

flat board   file cards   plywood reinforcement

keel   C-clamps

wooden strip baseboard

Figure 6. *Aligning the keel.*

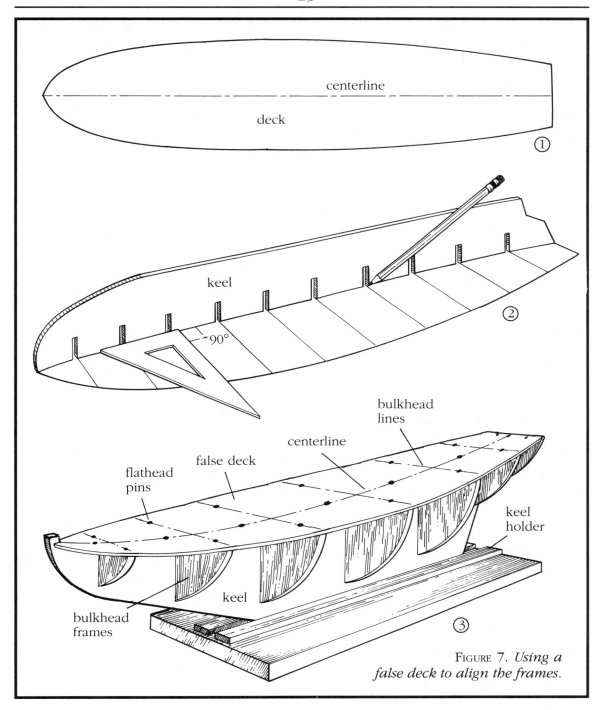

centerline

deck

①

keel

90°

②

bulkhead
lines

centerline

false deck

flathead
pins

keel
holder

keel

bulkhead
frames

③

FIGURE 7. *Using a
false deck to align the frames*.

in all cases success begins with a straight symmetrical hull.

The first and simplest technique uses the false deck itself to properly fit the frames. This system is found in Artesania Latina's *Swift* kit and in most other schooners. To begin, check the bulkhead frames and assemble the keel as we discussed earlier.

Figure 7 shows how we can use a false deck to align the frames. With a pencil, mark the centerline on both the top and bottom of the false deck **(1)**. Place the keel on the deck **(2)** and mark the outline of each of the frames' slots on the deck line. With a square, mark the bulkhead lines on both sides, and top and bottom, of the false deck. Next, assemble the bulkhead frames on the keel **(3)**.

Step 3 also shows a keel holder, which will hold the assembly in position and ensure that the keel is straight. Your keel holder will come in handy for more things than checking alignment — make one and hold on to it. The keel holder is made of flat scrapwood and two 3/8-inch by 1/2-inch strips as long as (or preferably a little longer) your hull. Sandwich the keel between the two strips and nail them to the board.

When assembling the bulkhead frames to the keel, make sure that:

- the center of each bulkhead is aligned with the keel.
- the tops of the frames are flush with the upper edge of the keel.

- the frames are neither too tight nor too loose in the keel notches.

Keep your hands off the glue, we're not ready yet.

Place the false deck on top of the frames and align its centerline with the keel **(3)**. Pin the deck to the top of the keel along its centerline, using flathead pins to avoid problems later with deck planking. Never force the deck onto the bulkheads, since this will produce distortions and buckling. Check the precut slots and file them to fit, as necessary. Pin the deck to the frames, following the bulkhead lines you marked in Step 1. Make sure every frame is exactly on its line under the deck; use two pins on each side of the centerline. To make this operation easier, clamp each frame in a vise as you drive the pins on top of it so that it is supported.

Now you're ready to glue the frames to the deck and keel. I use carpenter's glue right from the container. With a 1/4-inch brush, apply a bead of adhesive on the bow and stern side of each frame where it meets the deck and keel; every joint should be glued. Return the assembly to the keel holder to let the glue dry for at least 24 hours. The keel holder board will prevent distortions while the glue is curing.

FRAMES WITH BULWARK EXTENSIONS. Here's another type of construction, this time involving frames with bulwark extensions. Once you've assembled the

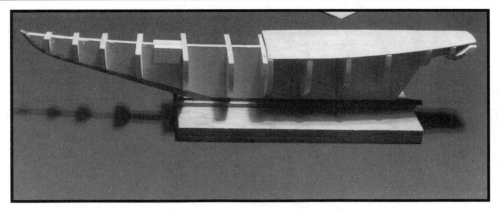

PHOTO 19. *The false deck will help align your framework. Note the blocks on the fifth bulkhead and how the tops of the bulkheads are flush with the top of the keel. Also note the keel holder, a piece of simple carpentry that will prove invaluable.*

keel and the frames — perfectly, of course — we are ready to proceed. In this case it would be very difficult to use the false deck to align and support the frames because most of these kits have precut frame slots that do not align perfectly.

Here's how I prefer to do it. Place the keel in the your keel holder board (see Step 3 in Figure 7) and check the frame to make sure that:

- the frame tops are flush with the upper edge of the keel.
- the frame bottoms are properly aligned fore and aft with the keel bottom.
- the frames do not fit too tightly on the keel
- the frame centers are exactly on the keel.

Next, remove all the frames from the keel. (No glue until everything is checked.)

Figure 8 illustrates what to do next. Set the midship frame in place and secure it with two square-edged pieces of scrapwood — glued to the keel on opposite sides of the keel against the midship frame **(1)**. This will ensure that the frame sits squarely on the keel and can serve as a guide for all others. Insert all the other frames in their slots and proceed as follows:

Take two strips of 3/8-inch by 1/8-inch scrapwood, lay them on top of the keel, and mark on them the center of all the keel's frame slots. Place the two strips on top of the frames as close to their edges as possible and pin the strips to the center frame. Now pin the strips to the rest of the frames following the frame

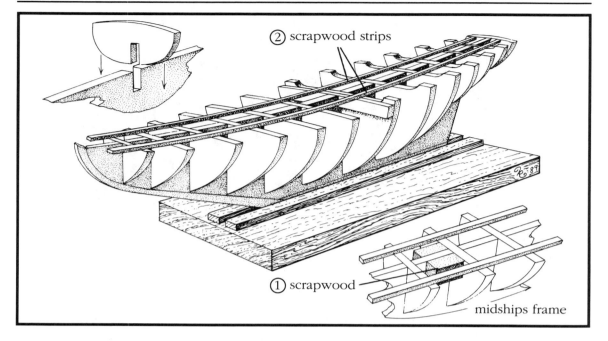

② scrapwood strips

① scrapwood

midships frame

FIGURE 8. *If the frame that will eventually become your hull isn't aligned properly, you might as well stop—nothing else will fit. There are a number of ways to make sure the frame's two components, the bulkheads and the keel, are fair and symmetrical. Fitting the bulkheads squarely into the keel slots might require blocks on the midship bulkhead and reinforcing strips pinned to the bulkhead tops.*

slot marks you just made **(2)**.

The distances between the marks will be exactly the same on both sides, so all the frames will be aligned and squared with the keel. Run a bit of glue along the joints where the frames meet the keel, set the assembly on the keel holder board, and let it dry thoroughly. The strips will be removed before installing the false deck.

KITS WITH PRECUT REINFORCING PIECES. Kits by Pan Art and Mamoli use precut

reinforcing strips that drop into slots cut in the bulkhead frames. This approach ensures a stronger hull and easier assembly. Figure 9 shows the method used by Pan Art in the *Amerigo Vespucci* kit. Here two precut reinforcing spacers running the length of the hull and fitting snugly into the frame slots do a nice job of holding the parts together **(1)**.

You'll still have a number of things to do to make sure the final assembly is distortion-free. A keel holder is once again the key to success.

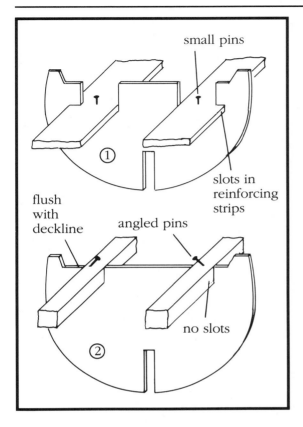

FIGURE 9. *Aligning frames with precut rein-forcing pieces.*

First, check all the bulkheads to make sure they fit properly in their positions on the keel. Next, set the midship frame on the keel and square it by installing two square-edged corner pieces (or right-angled triangular gussets, if you prefer), one on each side of the keel. Glue the corners and the bulkhead and keel and let them dry.

Now comes the task of checking that all the other bulkhead frames are fitted parallel to the midship frame. This is best accomplished by installing the frames one at a time. Add the next bulkhead on the keel and insert the two reinforcing spacers. The distances on each side of the keel between the midship frame and the new bulkhead should be the same. If they are, you know the two bulkheads are parallel. As you add more bulkheads, the distances should remain the same.

If this isn't true, or the spacers won't fit easily, proceed as follows:

File the slots in the spacers until the frame sets parallel to the center one, then fill in the gaps with thin wood strips until the fit is perfect.

Don't glue anything yet.

Now proceed with the rest of the bulkheads as previously explained. Everytime you check the next bulkhead, you will most likely have to remove the spacers and check how the cutouts fit on the bulkhead. It takes a little time and patience, but the final result will be worth your trouble.

When the bulkheads all are set in their stations with the spacers installed, you can drive in small pins to make sure everything stays in place. Now, with a thin brush, run a bit of carpenter's glue in all joints where the frames meet the keel and spacers. Install the assembly on the keel holder and let it dry.

The next method, illustrated in **(2)** and used by Mamoli for the *Constitution* kit, is similar to that shown in **(1)**, but is a little easier to work with. Start by checking the bulkheads and setting the midship bulkhead with the square reinforcing corners. The reinforcing strips in this method have no slots to fit the frames. Only a little filing may be required on the bulkhead slots to ensure that the reinforcing pieces fit into them. In this case it is most important that pins be used to keep the other bulkheads aligned with the midship bulkhead.

The reinforcing pieces in these kits are 10 mm square and it may be difficult to drive in the pins. Use a small bit to drill holes into the strips at the angles shown in **(2)** to make things easier. Make sure that the upper edges of the pieces don't extend above the deckline of the bulkheads. Once you're satisfied that all is square, glue away as we discussed previously.

Gunports

Manufacturers use a lot of approaches to cut and finish gunports. Some kits use precast frames, as shown in steps **(3)** through **(6)** in Figure 10; these are installed before the hull is planked. On other kits you'll simply cut through the planked hull, as in steps **(1)** and **(2)**. It's really a simple process once you understand how your kit addresses the problem.

I'll explain the whole process now, before you start planking. Gunports follow the rake of the deck, so while their upper and lower edges may be parallel

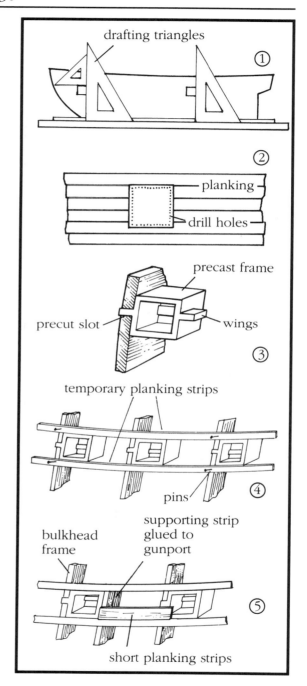

Figure 10. *Cutting the gunports.*

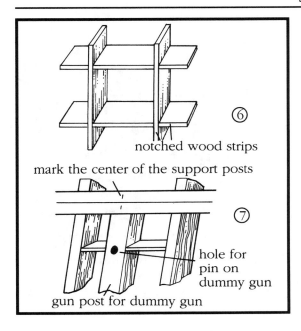

⑥

notched wood strips

mark the center of the support posts

⑦

hole for
pin on
dummy gun

gun post for dummy gun

FIGURE 10, CONTINUED. *Cutting the gunports.*

to the keel, their distances from the keel will vary: Make sure you consult the plans frequently and carefully.

Without frames:

The sides of the gunports must be square to their upper and lower edges. To do this, place the planked hull in your keel holder and set a drafting triangle alongside it **(1)**. Run the square along the keel holder and mark the sides of the gunports according to the plans. You can determine the position of each gunport by measuring the distance from the caprail to the upper side of the gunport on the plans. The gunports' upper and lower edges must be parallel to the base of the keel. Do this by placing a second square against the first one as shown in

Step 1.

To make the opening, drill a series of holes inside the lines you marked in Step 1 and cut across them with a sharp knife **(2)**. (When cutting and drilling gunports, it's a good idea to tape the inside of the bulwark so that the planking doesn't splinter.) A scalpel with a #11 blade works best. Rubbing the blade on a piece of wax will help ease the cut. Make several light cuts until the blade goes through, but don't use too much pressure or you'll crack the planks. Next, carefully file the edges to remove the drill marks.

Frame the sides of the gunports with wood strips (check your scale). I pick a different wood from what was used for the hull planking to obtain a contrast and bring out the framing.

With frames:

Mamoli kits use precast white metal gunport frames **(3)**. These have two wings: One, depending on where the gunport is located, is inserted and glued in a precut slot in the bulkhead. The other wing is then cut off.

There are some problems with this system. The slots in the bulkheads don't always line up, and their angle doesn't permit you to align the gunports with the hull. To overcome this I suggest the following: Pin a planking strip to the bulkhead frames in line with the bottom of the gunports **(4)**. Set each gunport frame on the strip; if the slots don't match, recut them and fill in with wood strips. Install another planking strip even with the upper edge of the ports. Now check that the ports will set flush with these two strips and glue the ports in place.

The plank ends at the gunports must be supported by a wood strip glued vertically just inside the port between the upper and lower planks **(5)**. The short planking strips between the gunports then can be glued to the supporting strip on one end and the bulkhead frame on the other. All this must be done carefully and with precision in order to preserve your smooth hull contour at the gunport level.

Movo uses wood strips notched into each other to form the gunport box **(6)**. This method is very accurate and easy to work with. The gunport frames are glued on precut bulwarks which are installed inside the bulkhead frames as each deck is built up. The outer edges of the gunport framing then must be faired and shaped to the contour of the two bulkheads on either side so that the planking between gunports can rest evenly on gunport frames and bulkheads. The best way of shaping the frames is to lay a file over their edges lengthwise along the hull and spanning the bulkheads. File gently to pare back the gunport frames. To be safe, apply a strip of masking tape to the edges of the bulkheads. When the file cuts the tape, it's time to stop.

On other models, you'll have to cut the gunports around the posts that will be used to support the dummy guns. The kit supplies a pattern with centerholes

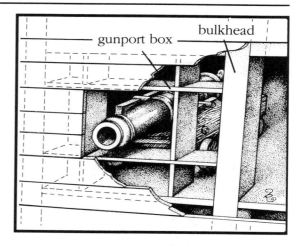

FIGURE 11. *Gunport frames must be cut and aligned with the bulkheads and the deck or you'll face the troubling possibility of skewed gun barrels and a cockeyed show of force.*

for the gunports' locations. Most of the time, the pattern isn't accurate and consequently, if you follow it, you'll end up with the ports in the wrong places. To avoid this problem, mark the center of the support posts **(7)** on the planks while you're planking. When you've finished the hull, you'll see where the posts are located.

PLANKING THE HULL AND DECK

PREPARATION

Now it's time to start planking the hull. While we're talking here about plank-on-bulkhead models, the same technique in a simpler form applies to solid hulls.

You'll need a six- to eight-inch high container filled with water, a plank bender (the electrically heated one made by Aeropiccola is very good. If you don't have a plank bender, you can use a hair-curling iron, although it won't work as well), an X-Acto knife with a #11 blade or a scalpel, a small hobby-type plane, a small hammer, a pair of needlenose pliers, a box of 1/2-inch brass pins, a drill with a bit slightly smaller than the diameter of the brass pins you're using, a small vise with a vacuum-type base, a metric ruler, a 12-inch steel or aluminum ruler, a block of wood 4 inches by 3/4-inch by 12 inches, white carpenter's glue, and ACC glue.

Scale will obviously affect the size of the planking you'll be using. Most 19th century ships rarely used deck planks wider than six inches; hull planking was wider, from eight to perhaps 12 inches on the real thing. At modelbuilding scale the difference is minuscule, but important. Maintaining authenticity means that you're going to be working with some very thin strips of wood.

Most kits contain two layers of planks: the first, or base planking, and the second, or finish planking. The first planking is generally light wood varying from 1 to 2 mm thick and 5 to 6 mm wide. The finish planking is generally walnut or oak, although occasionally it includes mahogany or other dark woods, or lime, which has a light yellow hue.

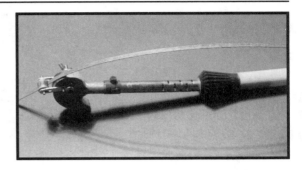

PHOTO 20. *An electric plank bender can make an exacting task a lot easier.*

Finish planking runs from 0.5 to 1 mm thick and from 3 to 5 mm wide. Make sure you're using the right planking. I've seen beginners install the finish planking as the base planking. The thinner finishing planks will not be strong enough to form a smooth, solid surface, and your efforts end up a big — and useless — mess.

Figure 12 will take us through the preparation stages. Follow these preparations meticulously before proceeding with the planking; the final outcome of the job will depend on it.

Before you begin actual planking, once again check the alignment of the frames. Step 1 shows the best way to make sure that the frames will provide a smoothly curving hull without unsightly humps or hollows. Temporarily pin three planking strips to each side of the hull assembly. When they are in place on three different levels (near the bulwarks, the waterline, and the keel), you can tell if some of the frames are too big or too

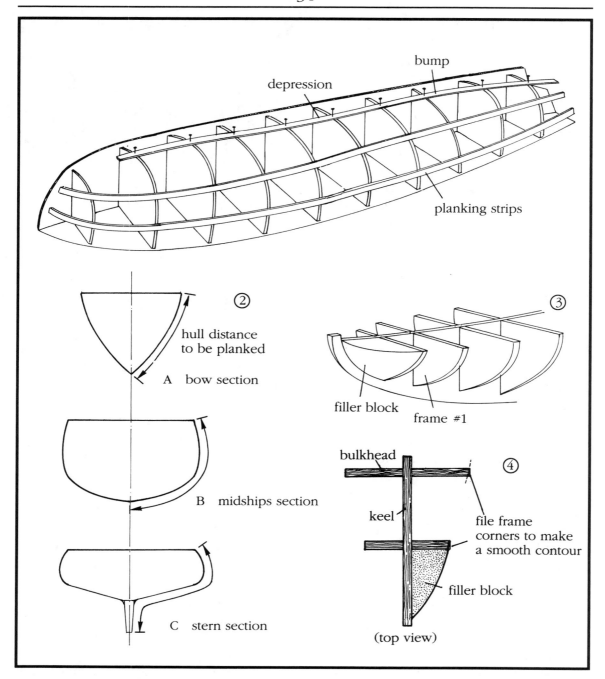

depression

bump

planking strips

② hull distance to be planked

A bow section

B midships section

C stern section

③ filler block

frame #1

④ bulkhead

keel

file frame corners to make a smooth contour

filler block

(top view)

FIGURE 12. *Preparing to plank the hull.*

small by the bumps or depressions in the strips. Fill the depressions by gluing 0.5mm-thick filler strips on the frame edge. Shave or file down the bumps until the strip runs in a smooth, fair curve over the frames. Shipbuilders call this "fairing" the frames; nowadays the process is aided by computer-generated patterns, but the old-timers always did their fairing by "rack of eye" when the frames were set up on the keel, much as we're doing it here.

Next, secure the hull in the vise by inserting the bottom of the midship frame in the vise jaws, and measure **(2)** the distances A, B. and C. Generally, A equals one-half of B, and C equals B plus a small amount.

Now it's time to take a deep breath and get ready for a little arithmetic. How do you get enough planks to cover B without creating a big jam at A or gaps at C?

The answer is tapering and filling.

The measured differences between A, B, and C will vary with the hull's shape, and will determine how to cut and install the planking. For example, if B is 140 mm, you would need 28 planks 5 mm wide (140 ÷ 5 = 28). In order to fit them all at A on the bow, you must consider the A measurement. If A equals one-half of B, then every plank must be tapered to end with one-half its original width, which, in this case, is 2.5 mm.

The taper on the forward end of the planks depends mostly on the shape of your hull; the measurements will vary slightly depending on the distance between A and B. Planks need to be tapered at the bow because they otherwise would ride up on each other and bulge as they follow the contour.

It's important that a filler block **(3)** be installed between frame #1 and the stempost to provide a solid surface for the end of the planks. Some kits include a small plywood piece you can glue against the keel and contour to the stempost, but in most cases it's too small to fill the gap and too thin to do any good. The filler block will provide a solid base on which to glue the planks. Saw a small piece of wood (pine is good) to roughly fit the gap; glue it in place; and file it down until it matches the contours of the edges of frame #1, the outline of the stem, and the outline of the deck. In addition, the edges of the forward frames must be filed **(4)** to follow the deck contour so the planks will lie on a flat surface and not on the corner of the frame.

The same procedure must be applied to the end frames of the stern. Here again, I prefer using a filler block to provide support for the planks.

Resist the urge to plank away and take the time to prepare the hull. Believe me, it'll make a major difference.

Now let's consider the stern measurement C. If C is bigger than B, you may need each plank's full width plus spacers inserted as wedges. Sometimes, paradoxically, you will need to taper the after ends of the planks *and* insert wedges, for reasons we'll examine later.

Planking the Hull — The First Layer of Planking

Before you do anything else, soak the planks for a couple of hours to make them more pliable and infinitely easier to work.

Figure 13 takes us through the proper planking procedure. Whether your kit has bulkheads that extend above the deck (to receive the bulwarks) or terminate flush with it, you must start the planking about one-half plank width below the deckline (1). This will provide a firm hold for your bulwark, as we will see later.

Before we get going, remember that when first fitting the planks to check the hull contour, we'll be pinning them to the frames temporarily. When everything checks out we'll use a gluing method that I'll explain shortly.

The first three or four planks (just how many will depend on the shape of the hull) will be pinned to the hull without tapering (temporarily, remember). On the bulkhead frames mark the distance down from the deckline where the first plank will be pinned. This will give you a clear idea of what's going to happen as the planks are fitted. You'll be able to see first, that all the planks ex-

tend the entire length of the hull, and second, where each will begin to twist upward as it adheres to the hull's contour.

All planks should be adjusted to the one immediately above it. Be careful: if the first plank isn't true, none of the others will be. Once that's in place, lay in the second plank with its top edge resting tightly against the bottom of the first, and pin it in place. Likewise for the third plank. On some models you may find that only one or two planks can be installed without tapering; it depends on the hull's contour — the rounder the shape, the more tapering you'll need.

Now we'll have to begin tapering. Position the fourth plank along the bottom edge of the third, starting from the middle of the hull and running toward the bow. You will notice that at Point X, the bottom plank will start to overlap the upper plank because of the bow curve. Mark that point (X) on the bottom plank and bend it over until it reaches the bow. The amount of overlap at the forward end will show how much this plank must be tapered. Mark the overlap and remove the plank from the hull.

Place your presoaked plank on a smooth wooden board (2) and lay your steel ruler along the line of overlap, beginning at Point X. I use an X-Acto knife with a #11 blade or a scalpel to cut the wedge of overlap. If the plank has been soaked awhile, the blade will cut into it quite easily. Never apply too much pressure by attempting to cut

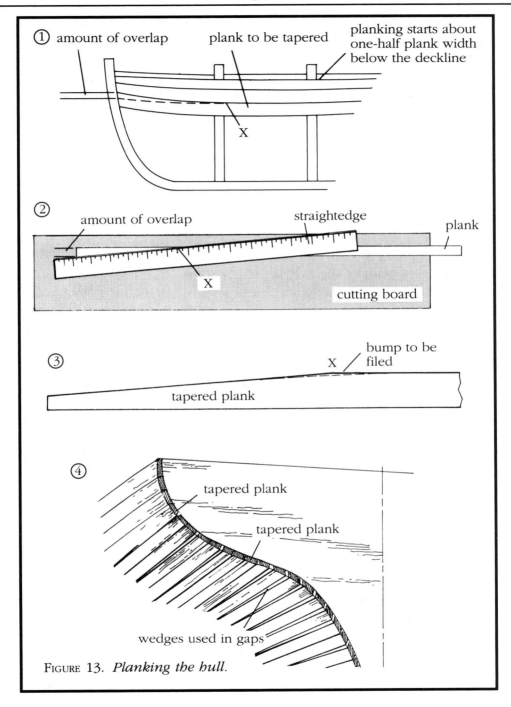

① amount of overlap   plank to be tapered   planking starts about one-half plank width below the deckline

X

② amount of overlap   straightedge   plank

X

cutting board

③ bump to be filed   X

tapered plank

④ tapered plank

tapered plank

wedges used in gaps

FIGURE 13. *Planking the hull*.

through in a single stroke. This will cause the plank to split. Instead, go over the cut a few times, gently applying pressure on the ruler. You will notice that after you cut the plank, there will be a bump **(3)** that must be filed down a bit. Save the wedges; they'll come in handy later, when we move to the ship's stern.

All planks must be bent. Next we will bend the tapered plank — and the first three untapered planks — to fit the curve of the hull. Using an electric plank bender, insert each plank in between the roller and the curved head of the bending machine and wait until the water turns into steam. Then gently bend the plank until the desired curve is obtained and the plank is dry.

To glue the first plank to the frames, mark the spots where the plank meets the frames. Drill small starter holes in the plank for the pins you're going to use and press one pin into each hole, but not all the way. With a small brush, apply a bit of carpenter's glue on the frames and on the filler block where the plank will rest. Apply a dot of ACC on the inside forward end of the plank and set the plank in place. Hold for about 15 seconds, and the plank will be anchored on this spot.

Next put some carpenter's glue on the upper edge of this plank. Leave a 1/2-inch glue-free gap in the center of each frame (Figure 14). Put a little ACC in these gaps. Then press the plank against the one above with your finger and push the pins partway in. The trick with this is to do one space at a time: carpenter's glue, gap, ACC, press and pin, then move on. The ACC will hold the planks together until the carpenter's glue is dry. The two planks will become firmly bonded without having to use clamps — and then having to wait as each plank dries. It's neat, it's easy, and it saves a lot of time.

Once the carpenter's glue dries, remove the pins. You can reuse them, and they won't be in the way when you sand the hull.

Some stern planks won't need to be tapered. But when they do, follow the procedure we used for tapering planks at the bow. Never force a plank out of its natural line; let it fall as it will over the frames, and taper as necessary. Check how the planks fit at the stern before gluing them in place. You will often find that you must leave a space [**(4)** in Figure 13] now and then, depending on the shape of the hull at the stern. These spaces will be filled with the wedges that you cut off at the bow end.

BULWARK BUILDING AND DECK PLANKING

Before we discuss planking decks or building bulwarks in detail, let's review the false deck installation. Earlier we discussed the basics of putting on the false deck in terms of using it to check the symmetry of the hull. Here's a re-

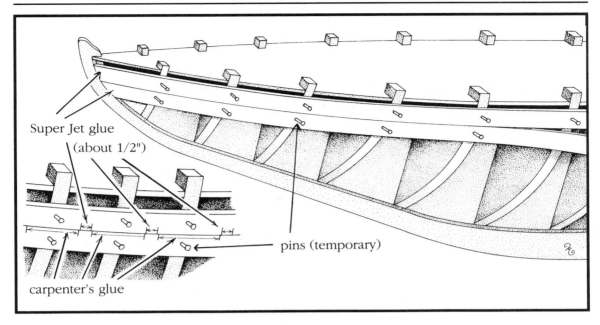

FIGURE 14. *Start planking the hull by temporarily pinning the upper plank just down from the deckline, not flush with it; this will give the bulwarks more purchase later. Spread carpenter's glue along the top edge of the second plank before fitting it, but leave a space midway between each bulkhead for strong Super Jet glue (ACC) for extra grip. The ACC will hold until the carpenter's glue kicks in: no clamping, no nailing, no fuss.*

minder, since this is an important process.

After all the bulkheads are glued in place, install the false deck (Figure 15). The precut slots must be checked and filed to fit as necessary. Never force the deck onto the bulkheads, since this will produce distortions and buckling. Once you've established that the fit is right, pin the deck across the tops of the bulkheads. Use flathead pins so that they won't interfere with the planking. After pinning down the deck, brush

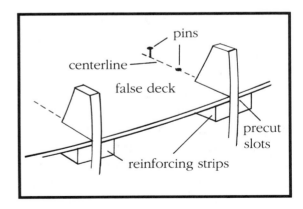

FIGURE 15. *Bulwark building and deck planking.*

carpenter's glue into the joints where the deck meets the bulkheads. Then secure the edges of the deck slots to the bulkheads. Use 3 mm by 3 mm reinforcing strips fastened with ACC. This will prevent the deck edge from bending.

THE BULWARKS. Plank-on-bulkhead kits use a variety of approaches to planking decks and building bulwarks. One bulwark method, used mostly by Artesania Latina, uses two precut strips of 3-ply sheet. Each strip is bent over the bulkheads then pinned to them along the deckline and glued at the sternpost, the bow, and along its lower edge to the first plank, which we installed below the deckline for this purpose. The problem with this is twofold: First, these bulwarks aren't planked inboard or outboard and simply don't look at all authentic; second, the bulwarks are too thin and will not cover the edges of the deck planking.

In this case my suggestion is also twofold. First, you can cover these plywood bulwarks using your own strips. (Check your scale; in most of the kits I've recommended, use 1 mm by 3 mm strips inboard and 1 mm by 4 mm outboard.) Second, you can discard the plywood bulwarks and build your own.

Here are two alternatives for building bulwarks — and either works quite well. The first one — if your model has bulkhead extensions — calls for first installing outboard planks horizontally following the above-deck extensions of

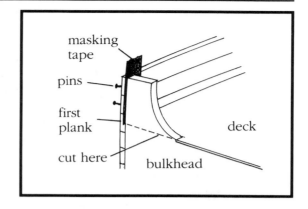

FIGURE 16. *Bulkhead extensions provide an excellent base for bulwark planking.*

the bulkheads. Then the bulkhead extensions are cut off at deck level and the inside is planked with horizontal strips overlapping the outside planks (see Figures 16 and 18). As an alternative, you can install outboard planks horizontally as in the first method, then cut off the bulkheads' extensions, and install inboard vertical planking to be sandwiched between another set of inboard horizontal planks. This makes for a very solid bulwark. Let's detail the procedure, which is similar, in both cases.

Start by covering the edges of the bulkheads above the deck with masking tape (Figure 16) to prevent the planks from being glued to the extensions (which we'll want to remove later). The first plank must follow the deckline and be pinned and glued to the bulkhead below the tape. Install it half the width above the deckline to receive the lower half of the first inboard plank. Glue the next three outboard planks to each other using the clamp-free method I discussed on page 38. Don't glue them to the tape on the exterior face of the bulkheads; just pin them there temporarily. Remember *not* to push the pins in all the way; you're going to pull them out later. After everything is set, cut off the bulkhead extensions above the deck. I use my X-Acto minisaw here, bending the handle upward slightly for convenience as I cut. Now you can plank the deck before planking the bulwarks inboard.

THE DECKS. Kits will contain strips for planking the deck, but if you'd like to improve your model's finished appearance, use your own stock — like 1 mm by 3 mm boxwood or a similar, good-quality wood. The strips are generally cut in two lengths: 80 mm and 40 mm. If you're going to supply your own stock, here's a quick way to get out those lengths from longer strips. The jig shouldn't take more than five minutes to build.

Find a flat, square-edged board, a foot or so long by 4 or 5 inches wide — it doesn't have to be precise. On the face of this board, near one end, tack a short strip of scrapwood. This strip should be straight, true, and square-edged but needn't be any particular size; a strip 3 to 4 inches long tacked across a board 4 to 5 inches wide would work fine. This will become the base of your plank-cutting jig. Now find a thin piece of scrapwood with straight, flat edges. From that

PHOTO 21. *Cutting your own deck planks can be a breeze if you've got five minutes to put together a jig: no need for time-consuming measuring or marking; just slip in a plank and cut away.*

cut a 40 mm strip and an 80 mm strip. Be accurate; the ends must be cut squarely and cleanly. Erect these two strips side by side on your base, making sure their ends are butted squarely against it, and pin them to the board. The result is an inverted "T" with two stems. Butt the end of a planking strip against the T's base and edge-set it against the 80 mm stem, grab your knife, and cut: You have a quick and clean 80 mm plank. The same for the 40 mm side.

Once you've built up a supply of planks it's time to begin. Draw a line in the center of the false deck from bow to stern. Starting at the stern, glue a 40 mm strip along and to one side of the centerline, then continue that row of planking with 80 mm strips glued end to end

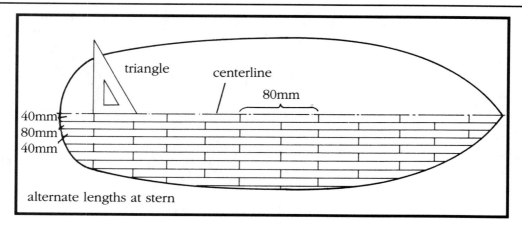

FIGURE 17. *A properly planked deck calls for a staggered look.*

toward the bow (Figure 17). The forwardmost plank will have to be cut from either a 40 mm or 80 mm strip, depending on its length. Plank subsequent rows from stern to bow moving toward each bulwark, alternating 40 mm and 80 mm strips at the stern to achieve a staggered look in the finished planking. If the stern is curved, cut the aftmost 40 mm strips so their forward ends are aligned with one another across the deck, and do the same for the aftmost 80 mm strips. I usually draw a line with a triangle where the ends of the first row of planks must stop.

To add authenticity to the deck use a small nail or tack to make two indentations at the corners of each plank. Smooth the deck with fine sandpaper; the sawdust will collect in the indentations. Apply a coat of acrylic matte varnish (Liquitex is good). The sawdust collected in the indentations will darken,

simulating nail heads in the deck. When the varnish dries go over the deck with fine (0000) steel wool to finish things up.

Once you've laid the deck you can start the inboard planking for the bulwarks. There are two ways to install the inboard planking. The first is to lay horizontal strips as we did on the outboard side (Figure 18). The lower end of the first plank will rest on the deck planking, giving a perfect finish to the job, and it will overlap the outboard planking, providing structural strength. Since we started a half plank higher on the inboard side, the final inboard plank will have to be sliced in half lengthwise to even things out.

Step **2** shows an alternative. Two rows of planks are installed inboard of the bulwarks; the first row runs vertically, adding more strength to the structure. Be sure that the lower ends of the planks are also glued to the deck. The second

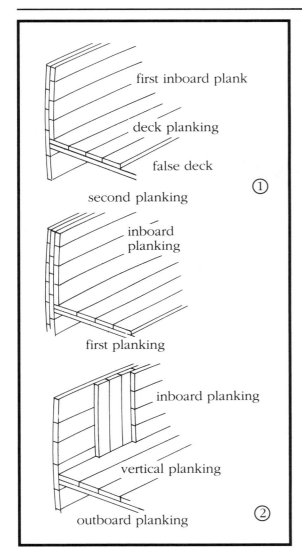

first inboard plank

deck planking

false deck

second planking

①

inboard planking

first planking

inboard planking

vertical planking

outboard planking

②

FIGURE 18. *The inboard sides of the bulwarks can be planked in a number of ways for both strength and attractiveness.*

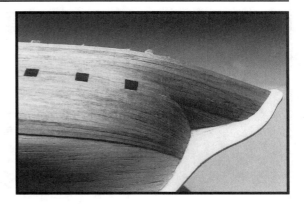

PHOTO 22. *Tapered, snug, and smooth, the half-completed layer of second planking on this model of the* Constitution *shows how exacting a process is involved.*

SECOND LAYER OF HULL PLANKING

The second or finished planking is generally done with the 0.5 mm by 3 mm or 0.5 mm by 4 mm walnut strips supplied in the kits. Some manufacturers include two kinds of wood strips to give the model a more attractive look. On some kits, you'll want to paint the hull below the waterline and leave wood natural above it. Whatever the case, the method of installing the planks is the same.

The first planking must be finished and treated to ready the hull for installation of the second planking. Check that the plank edges are even, and use a wood file to level any rough spots. Next, sand the entire hull surface, then apply a coat of modeling paste (Hyplar or Liquitex are two good products), which you can buy at any art supply store. This will

row of planks runs horizontally. This system is also used when gunports must be cut through the bulwarks.

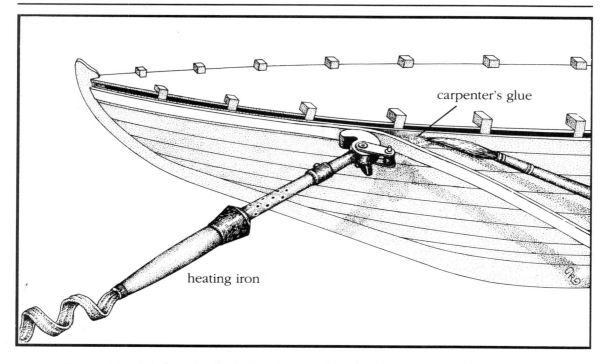

carpenter's glue

heating iron

FIGURE 19. *An electric plank bender supplies the heat, a paint brush applies the glue — the hull begins to take shape. The second layer of planking can be applied more easily using the heat of the plank bender, though not its bending capability. While not illustrated here, the second planking is best applied after the bulwarks have been built.*

give the hull a smooth, tough coat to hold the planks together. It will also provide a good base for your second planking and won't absorb the glue, thus making it dry too quickly. Once the paste is dry, sand the hull and you're ready to begin.

As with the first planking, the second planking must be tapered. Start at the caprail and proceed all the way to the keel. This time you'll have the experience of the first planking to guide you.

You'll be able to tell where and how you made mistakes and correct them. There is one difference, though: *No nails or pins are used on the second planking, even temporarily.*

Figure 19 shows how to apply the planking by using glue and heat. Taper and bend each plank as you did with the first layer, checking that the plank fits tightly and smoothly on the hull — no bumps. With a brush, dab a bit of white carpenter's glue as wide as the plank and no more than 4 or 5 inches in length on the forward end of the hull where the plank will sit. Next, apply about 1/2 inch of ACC to the tip of the plank at the bow, position it, and hold it for about 15 seconds until the adhesive sets. Now place the plank in the carpenter's glue. Push up with one thumb to make sure it's a very tight fit and that no cracks are left between planks.

At the same time, apply heat to the plank by using the plank bender in a back-and-forth motion with your left hand. This evaporates the water in the glue for a faster set, steams the plank, and forms it to the curve of the hull — everything you need to ensure a perfect bond. Do only a few inches at a time; otherwise the carpenter's glue will dry before you can press the plank to it. Continue gluing toward the stern, where you must finish at the end of the plank with another 1/2 inch of ACC. Leave the plank ends extending past the stern; you can cut them later. Any fillers should also be applied using heat from the plank bender.

When all the planking is finished, check for any small cracks or spaces left between the planks. Apply a little carpenter's glue to these places and smooth with very fine sandpaper. The sanding dust will stick to the glue and cover every small imperfection. Sand the rest of the hull and finish with a coat of acrylic matte varnish, just as we did with the deck. When it's dry, rub it gently with a very fine (0000) steel wool pad. The process will leave a luster-free natural finish.

HANDLING ITEMS ON DECK

GUNS

INSTALLATIONS ON OPEN DECKS. The guns supplied in kits for open decks normally are installed on wood or metal mounts of the truck or sled type, as in Mamoli's *Constitution*.

Because of the intricacy of rigging guns — breeching ropes, side and train tackles, all with accompanying blocks — the process of gun rigging can be quite tricky, tedious, and time-consuming. Figure 20 illustrates the end result of a method that will make this job simpler. The trick is keeping the gun away from the model until the more delicate rigging is finished.

To start with, you must use very small blocks, single or double as called for in the plans. Most kits don't supply blocks small enough for this job — 1/16 inch or 3/32 inch for most of the models I've suggested — but you can buy them; some are already *stropped* (banded by rope or iron). Install one block on each side of the carriage for the side tackles and two on the back for the train tackles. Put the gun aside for a minute and tie a block to a ringbolt; the ringbolt will be installed on the bulwark. Next, tie the

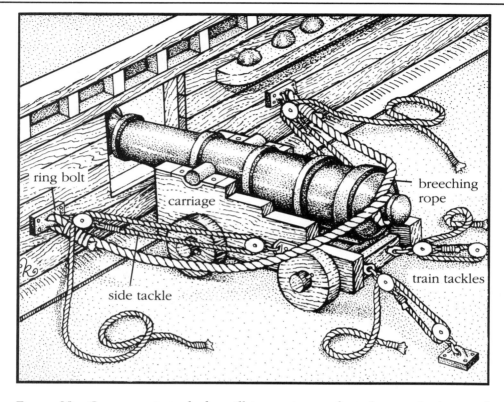

FIGURE 20. *Guns on open decks will present your first shot at rigging and handling blocks—a tricky, and tension-inducing interlude. Don't worry, there are ways to make it easy. Separate your tasks into stages that will allow you to rig small blocks before the gun is installed on deck.*

side tackle rope to the block's *becket* (the eye on the bottom). Repeat for the other side tackle. Also tie the breeching rope to one ringbolt (it doesn't matter which) and leave the other end loose for the time being. Now install the ringbolts with the blocks and the ropes on the bulwark as shown in Figure 20.

Next install the gun on the *carriage* (the bed for the gun), place some glue on the bottom of the wheels and on the front of the carriage, and set the gun assembly in place against the port. After the glue dries, you're ready to rig the tackles.

Start with the side tackles. Thread the rope through the block on the gun mount and back through the block on the bulwark. Let the end of the tackle coil on the deck and secure it with a bit of glue. Use a needle threader to feed the rope through the blocks. Next, secure the

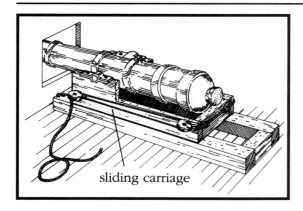

sliding carriage

FIGURE 21. *A gun on a sled carriage — easier to rig than others.*

breeching rope — a heavy rope that absorbed the recoil of the gun — by using a pair of tweezers to twist the rope around the back pin on the gun barrel while pulling it through the opposite ringbolt; then apply a dab a ACC on the ring. Now rig the train tackles as shown.

This procedure simplifies the gun rigging operation because it eliminates the need to tie ropes to ringbolts on the bulwark after the gun is set in place. There is no room to work in those very tight spots.

The sled-type carriage is simpler to rig because the side tackles aren't mounted on the bulwark rings, but on the front of the sled train. These tackles can be rigged on the gun mount before it's glued in place (Figure 21). The breeching rope is installed following the same procedure used for the truck-type gunmount.

COVERED DECKS. For the covered decks, the guns may be full-length barrels or dummy types. The dummy guns are pinned on the posts installed in the framework during the hull assembly (see Figure 10), and the full-length ones will be set with glue on their mounts, which are installed with glue and pins on the lower decks during the hull construction. In both cases, the guns are worked in place through their ports. It's a good idea to tie a temporary string to the end of each barrel, so that if the gun falls inside during installation you can get it back.

PIN RACKS AND PIN RAILS

There is nothing more frustrating than a rack that splits open or pulls off the deck or bulwark when you're belaying a line. At that point in construction, it's nearly impossible to replace or repair the broken part. That's why it's very important that these racks be made of strong wood and installed solidly. Here's the rub: most of the wood strips supplied in kits are weak and inadequate. To overcome this, and to be on the safe side, I normally use either boxwood or holly (which you can buy from hobby mail order catalogs). These woods are practically grainless and very strong. Stain them as needed. As a second choice you could use maple or oak. Figure 22 shows some tips for ensuring solid construction.

The fife rails located at the bases of the masts should have overlapping and notched joints; they should never be

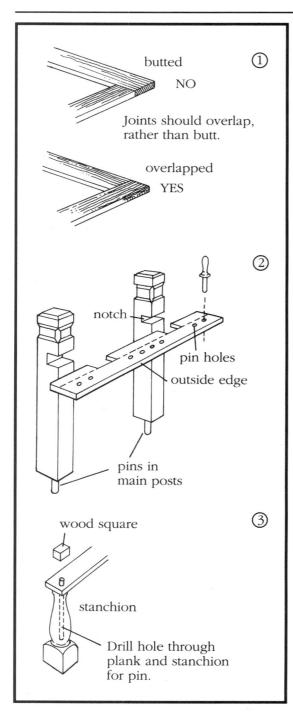

butted **(1)**. Make sure the corners are square.

The notches on the headposts of the belaying pin racks **(2)** must be cut precisely so that the planks fit snugly into them. A loose joint will break easily when you belay the lines to the pins. The holes for the pins should be drilled close to the outside edge of the plank to make it easier to belay ropes.

Most kits supply wooden belaying pins. Even if they look more authentic, generally they're too thick and out of scale. Since there is rarely enough space on the rack to accommodate the number of pins required, you'll end up setting the pins too close to each other and you won't be able to turn your lines around them. You can overcome this problem by using brass pins, available from hobby suppliers.

When installing the pins in the holes, make sure to apply a bit of glue to their stems. This practice will prevent the pins from popping out when you try to belay a rope.

The short posts or stanchions must be drilled through. Insert a brass pin through the plank, through the stanchion, and down into the deck **(3)**. Apply glue to the top and bottom of the stanchion and on the pin. You can glue a small square of wood over the head of the pin to hide it. I also drill up into the bottom of each main post, cut the head off a

FIGURE 22. *Building pin racks and pin rails.*

brass pin, apply some glue, and insert the pin in the hole. This pin will puncture the deck to secure the post.

DECKHOUSES

Deckhouse walls are made mostly of thin plywood, which doesn't provide enough surface for gluing at the corners. This can lead to an out-of-square deckhouse. Figure 23 shows how to correct this.

Along and flush with the ends and top edges of the two side walls glue three strips of 3 mm by 3 mm wood **(1)**. These will strengthen the plywood and provide a good surface for gluing the forward and after walls **(2)**. Next, cut a scrapwood block to fit snugly between the end pieces. This piece should have square corners, which will ensure that the house is squared. Temporarily pin the side walls to the block, check for squareness, then glue and pin the end panels onto the reinforcing strips we installed in **(1)**.

When the adhesive is dry, remove the pins and the wood block and finish the roof and sides as needed. Since the deck is cambered athwartships with its crown along the fore-and-aft centerline, it's necessary to introduce some concavity to the bottoms of the forward and after walls of the deckhouse **(3)**. One way to do this is to pin a piece of sandpaper to the deck over the site on which the house will sit. Rub the house lengthwise back and forth over the sandpaper until its bottom edges match the camber of the deck. Now remove the sandpaper and

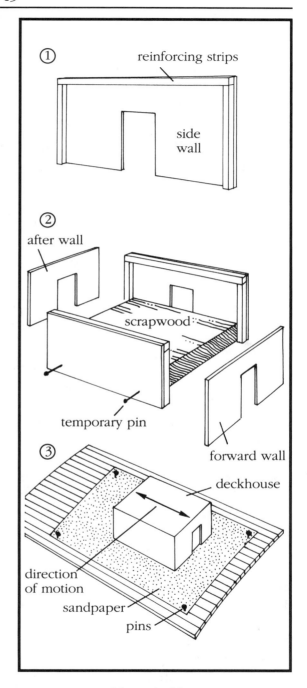

FIGURE 23. *Building deckhouses.*

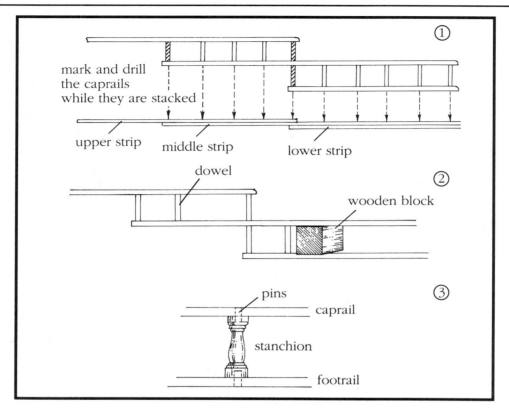

mark and drill
the caprails
while they are stacked

upper strip   middle strip   lower strip

①

dowel

wooden block

②

pins

caprail

stanchion

footrail

③

FIGURE 24. *Producing strong handrailings.*

glue the house to the deck. The same procedure can be used when building companionways, skylights, or other parts that must be fitted to a curved surface.

Railings and Stanchions

Bulwarks and handrailings on period ships built from kits are mostly made of wood strips and wood *stanchions* — the vertical supports. The most challenging part of this construction is to produce a strong, well-aligned finished product.

Figure 24 illustrates a few methods to simplify this important task.

The railings with straight stanchions are made by using thin dowels inserted in holes drilled through two rails. You can see a stepped combination of railings running from stem to stern in **(1)**. This type of railing is found on more ornate ships such as the *San Felipe.*

To ensure an accurate alignment of stanchions, it's necessary to drill the holes in the strips while they're stacked together in the position they'll assume on the bulwarks. To do this, cut the lower or shorter strip to fit its position on the model, then cut the middle strip and mark on both strips the vertical axes along which the lower and middle strips will connect. Hold the two strips together with an alligator clip, aligning the mark. Next cut the upper strip, set it on top of the middle strip, and align its end with the connecting axis for all three strips. Clip the middle and upper strips together. Now the point at which all three strips will be connected has been located and marked.

Next, mark the hole centers for the stanchions on the upper and middle strips and drill them. Separate the strips and glue them in place where they overlap the bulwarks, making sure they are properly aligned at their free ends. To do this, insert one dowel for each strip while gluing them in place **(2)**. When the adhesive is dry, affix the rest of the stanchions in their holes. To ensure accurate vertical spacing between the rails, use a block of wood cut to the correct height to check for discrepancies.

In another type of railing, the stanchions aren't set in predrilled holes. Using the method explained in **(1)** and **(2)**, drill pin holes in the strips. Next, drill pin holes on both ends of the stanchions and glue pins into them **(3)**. Cut the pins to the rail's thickness. Now install the footrail on the ship. Place a dab of glue on the bottom end of each stanchion and insert the pin in the appropriate footrail hole. When the stanchions are in posi-

tion, apply glue to their tops. Using a pair of tweezers, line up the pins with the handrail holes and set the handrail in place.

Some railings can be assembled off the deck and then installed in one piece. You can cover the handrail with a thin strip of the same kind of wood as the railing, or with a different type for contrast.

CHANNELS (CHAIN WALES) AND DEADEYES

Chain wales (pronounced and referred to henceforth as "channels") and deadeyes secured the shrouds to the hull. Your kit should contain the materials needed to make and install these fixtures, which will vary in size, shape, and arrangement depending on the model you're building.

It makes the most sense to install the channels and the deadeyes before setting the hull on its permanent display base. This allows you to tilt the hull to one side and work more easily. (See Figure 26.)

You'll find that some channels have holes for the passage of the chainplates **(1)**; some have notches cut along the edges and covered with wooden strips **(2)**; some ships will have double channels **(3)**; and some will have segmented channels to straddle the gunports **(4)**. Some ships will have wider channels, while others, such as schooners, will have none at all.

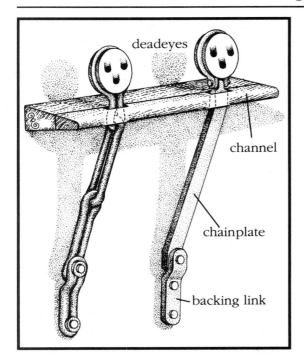

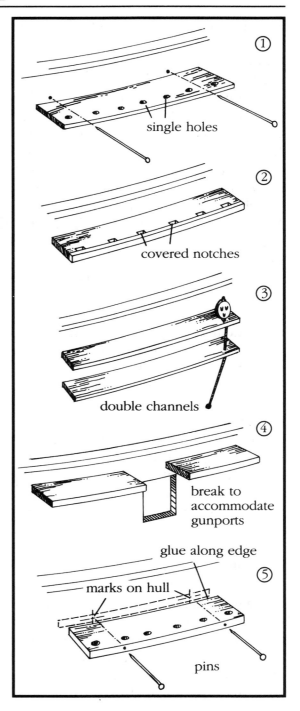

FIGURE 25. *Deadeyes, channels, and chain-plates: simple, succinct, and functional engineering. Shrouds supporting the masts are belayed via lanyards to the deadeyes, which are secured to the outboard surface of the hull by chainplates. Channels prevent the shrouds from chafing the side of the ship and provide an extended base of support for the masts.*

Install the channels using both glue and pins **(5)**. Drill the pin holes (*very slow speed*, with the channels in a vise or drill stand) through the channels between where the chainplate rods will pass, insert the pins, put the channel in

FIGURE 26. *Installing channels and deadeyes.*

its position, and tap the pins gently to mark the hull. Remove the channel and drill small holes at the marks. Apply glue to the edge of the channel, line up the pins with the holes, and tap down the pins. Cut off the pinheads for a better look.

When positioning the channels, make sure that neither the shrouds nor the chainplates fall in front of your gunports (Figure 27). Hold the channels in place temporarily and study the gunport pattern so that you can mark the chainplate holes in their proper location (**1** and **2**).

The chainplates must be aligned with the shrouds. To accomplish this properly, insert a dowel in the mast hole. Mark the height of the masttop (your plans should indicate the mast's height) on the dowel and tie a string to it. Run the string through each of the chainplate holes and mark the spot where the chainplate will be pinned (**3**). You can use a strip of tape to mark the horizontal line along which the pins will be positioned. The height of the tape will depend on the length of the chainplates, which varies from one kit to another.

Some chainplates can be made by wrapping a wire around the deadeye as you would a block and twisting the wire until the proper length is obtained (Figure 28). Then you cut off one end of the wire and wrap the other around the pin (**1**). With other kits, you make the chainplates from preshaped wires. Be aware that with this type of chainplate, the ends

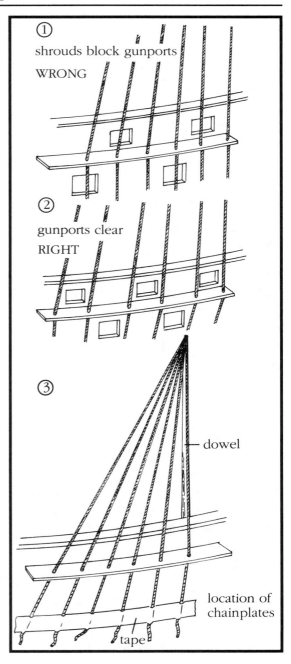

Figure 27. *Carelessly installing channels can come back to haunt you later.*

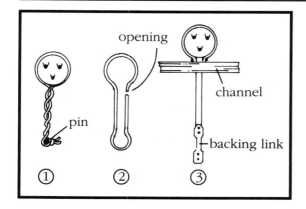

FIGURE 28. *Different types of chainplates, not all of them useful.*

that wrap around the deadeyes are open and will lose their grip when you adjust the shrouds. Maybe a dab of glue will help, but I don't suggest using these chainplates **(2)** — the potential for a mess is high.

On some models the chainplates end with a backing link. This is a brass plate installed on the hull to strengthen the anchorage of the chainplate **(3)**.

Some kits supply chainplates made from tempered brass strips. The tempering makes them very hard to bend without breaking, and very difficult to drill. One handy trick is to place these strips over a gas flame until they turn red, then let them cool. This will soften the brass and make it much easier to handle.

MARKING THE WATERLINE

WATERLINE MARKING JIG. One of the things that really can make you stop and

scratch your head in puzzlement is marking the waterline. Any number of methods have been suggested in books and kit instructions — you can even buy a factory-made jig in hobby shops. Here's a way to save yourself some money by grabbing a few scraps of wood and quickly building a jig. And it works great every time.

To build the jig shown in Figure 29, all you need is: one 26-inch-long strip of wood 1/2 by 2 inches, and one 6-inch-long strip 1/2 by 3-1/2 inches; any type of saw; one 1/4-inch by 1-1/4-inch bolt with a wingnut and washer; your drill; some #4 finishing nails; a piece of felt; a fine-point marker; soft wire; and a half-hour of your time.

Cut the 26-inch strip into five pieces in the lengths (A, B, C, D, E) shown in Figure 30. (The extra inch allows for cutting waste.) Cut a 1/4-inch-wide slot on piece C as shown. Drill a 1/4-inch hole in piece D, 1 inch from its end. Mark a centerline on piece A and drill four 1/32-inch holes, two on each side of the line and parallel to each other. These holes are needed to insert the soft wire to hold the marker in place. The wires are then twisted on the other side with pliers as shown in Figure 29.

Take a look at Figure 29 to see how it all fits together. You can raise or lower the marker to match the height of your model, and its base will slide easily.

MARKING THE WATERLINE. Now let's move on to marking the waterline, which

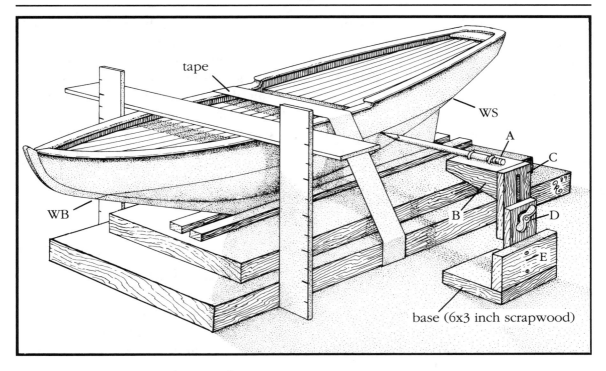

FIGURE 29. *Waterline marking jig.*

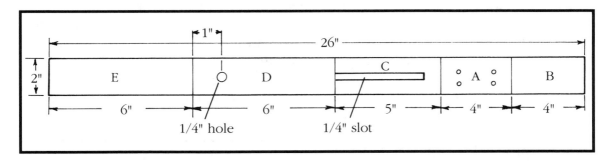

FIGURE 30. *Proper cuts for the waterline marking jig.*

calls for some more construction as we can see in Figure 29. To ease the strain, find a base to raise your model and the keel holder about 5 inches above the table. I flip over an empty cardboard box for my base. You'll also need two rulers, a straight wood strip, and tape.

Set your model on the board and base as shown in Figure 29. Set the wood strip across the bulwarks and measure the height on either side with rulers placed directly across from one another to port and starboard. Level the hull until the measurements are equal. Tape the hull to the base and recheck the measurements.

Next, find the height of the waterline above the bottom of the keel. This distance (measured upward from the keel) is either given or can be measured from the profile view of the ship on your plans. Assuming the keel bottom of your model parallels the waterline, simply adjust your jig to the waterline height and run the marker along both sides of the hull. It's as easy as that.

On many hulls (Baltimore clippers and fishing schooners, for example), the keel doesn't run parallel to the waterline, but rather is deeper aft than forward (the keel is said to have "drag" in such instances). The long, sloping forefoot running from stem to keel on the fishing schooner is a further complication. In such instances you'll have to raise the model at the bow to obtain the proper position the waterline there.

To determine the exact position of WB (waterline at the bow) in such an instance, proceed as follows: On your plan, draw a line along the keel bottom (this represents your keel holder), extending it forward. Measure the distance from WB to the line. Note the distance, move to the model, place the square on the keel holder, and mark WB. Move back to the plans and do the same thing for WS (waterline at the stern).

Now that we have WS and WB marked on the model, take the jig and set it on WS. Move the jig to the bow and raise the bow until WB matches the height of the marker. Slide a spacer under the hull, tape the hull down as we did in Figure 29 before, and run the jig along both sides. You'll have a beautiful waterline.

SETTING THE HULL ON THE DISPLAY BASE

When you've finished the hull — planking, decks, deck fittings, channels, deadeyes, railings, deck blocks, waterline — it's time to install it permanently on the display base. We do this before stepping (setting) the masts and the bowsprit. Leave the boat davits for later, or they'll get in your way while you're rigging.

Kits supply several types of display bases, including wooden cradles set on

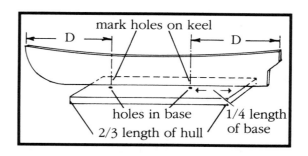

FIGURE 31. *Setting the hull on the base.*

a precarved wood base and brass stanchions set on a wood base, or launching ways on a wood base. The choice is yours, although some bigger models are steadier on solid wood cradles than on brass stanchions. In any case it is important to secure the bigger models with screws.

The base should be approximately two-thirds the total length of the hull, with the supports set about one-quarter of the way in on each end. Mark, then drill the holes for the base, using a drill bit the exact size of the screws. (Use #6 wood screws.) Turn the base over and countersink the holes in its bottom. Set the hull in place with the keel near the holes and make sure that the distances (D) are as equal as possible (Figure 31). Now mark the holes' centers on the side of the keel.

Set the hull on its side, mark the hole centers with an awl under the keel, and drill pilot holes for the screws up into the keel. Keep the drill bit square with the keel while drilling.

You will need help to set and fasten the hull on the base. Set the base on the corner of a table with its end hanging off. Have someone hold the hull while you set it on the stanchions and screw it in place from below. If you decide to use a wooden cradle instead of brass or wood stanchions, refer to the bulkhead shapes from your drawings.

If you wish, you can make launching ways from square wood stock or buy them from your distributor, but again you must secure your model to the base with wood screws.

When the hull (with its decking fixtures such as belaying pins, cleats, ringbolts, guns and their rigging) is finished, put it aside and cover it with plastic to keep it safe and free from dust until you're ready to install the completed masts. Do not fit the masts or the bowsprit until later.

PART III

Masting and Rigging

"The rigging of a ship consists of a quantity of Ropes, or Cordage, of various dimensions, for the support of the Masts and Yards. Those which are fixed and stationary, such as Shrouds, Stays, and Back-stays, are termed Standing Rigging; *but those which reeve through Blocks, or Sheave-Holes, are denominated* Running Rigging; *such as Haliards, Braces, Clew-lines, Buntlines, &c. &c. These are occasionally hauled upon, or let go, for the purpose of working the Ship."*

— The Young Sea Officer's Sheet Anchor, *1819*

GETTING STARTED

The quest for the perfect blend of masts and sails began the moment it dawned on primitive mariners that they could harness the wind and — sans sweat — move their boats through the water. The evolution continues today, with sailors using computer-designed sails and modern alloy spars to squeeze the most from wind and craft.

Cutting the waves on a downwind run, the first sailor likely had no idea why the animal skin he hung to catch the wind was pushing him along. The physical principles behind the concept of using wind and sail to produce motion are simple. But adapting those principles has led to a chase that will give aspiring model builders an infinite variety of styles to pursue.

Animal skins eventually gave way to more pliable materials — papyrus, and flax, then woven cloth. And as boats became bigger, so too did the sails — which sailors expanded by sewing strips

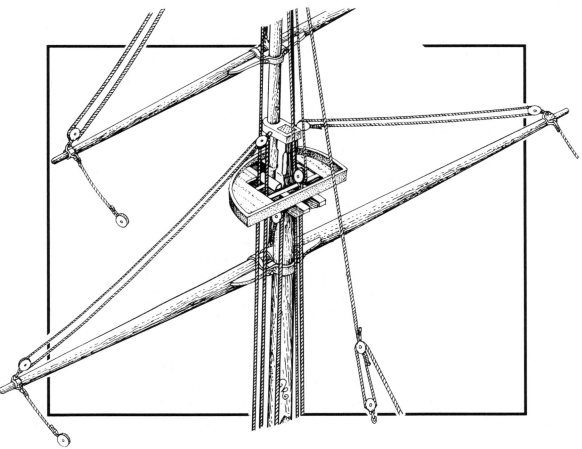

of cloth together. Canvas became the cloth of choice. To strengthen the sail in high winds, a rope was sewn around its edges. Seamen ran ropes through eyelets in the sail's corners to hold it in place, or adjust it to the ship's advantage.

To hold the sail up to the wind, shipwrights used wooden (later steel) poles called *yards*. The yards were held in the air by bigger poles, or *masts*.

To secure the masts and the yard — which together with *booms*, *gaffs*, and *sprits* are collectively called *spars* — shipwrights developed *standing rigging*. Standing rigging includes *stays*, which secure masts fore and aft, and *shrouds*, which do the same athwartships. To enable seamen to climb the mast to furl or unfurl the sails, rope ladders, or *ratlines*, were tied to the shrouds.

The spars and canvas were knitted together by ropes — *running rigging* — that moved the yards and the sails not only up and down but at different angles to the ship to catch the wind on different headings. The weight of the yards and the force of the wind became too much to handle, so the ropes (or, more properly, *lines*) were rigged through wooden *blocks* with *sheaves* (pronounced "shivs") to produce *tackles*. These reduced the amount of power needed to pull against a weight or opposing resistance. The more times a line is rigged over sheaves (i.e. the more *parts* in the tackle), the less power is needed to overcome the weight at the other end. So on a ship's rigging we will find tackles with blocks having one, two, or more sheaves.

To secure the ends of all this running rigging, early ships used shaped pieces of timber called *bitts, cavils*, and *cleats*. Later, as the sailing apparatus became more and more complicated and more line ends needed to be secured, *belaying pins* were fashioned and inserted into holes drilled in *belaying pin racks, pin rails*, or *fife rails*, so called because the fifer — flute player — often sat there. His playing helped ease the crew's burden as they sweated the great yards aloft.

To successfully mast and rig a model you'll need to understand the function of every part involved. As a general rule you can assume that the basic function of masts and rigging is essentially the same on every sailing ship. Any differences are stylistic adaptations to suit a particular environment or task. For example, yard braces — which controlled the sail's angle to the wind — were invariably rigged from the yard ends and

brought down to belay on the deck below. But in a man o'war — a fighting ship with a need to keep its bulwarks (and guns) free of a lot of lines — these braces were brought first to a block fixed on a stay, then to a lower block, and then to the belaying pin rack. On a clipper ship (which had no guns to man), the braces were fed through a block on an adjacent mast, and then brought down to the belaying pin rack.

Once you know that a yard has to have two braces, you'll know what to look for in plans and how to rig them on your model. Just remember this: You're now about to start a very delicate and exacting phase of building your model; it's easy to make frustrating mistakes. Be patient. If you suddenly find yourself entwined in a mess of line you hoped would be your ratline assembly, take a deep breath and a step back.

If you follow the steps outlined in this section, you'll be able to mast and rig any model. Believe me, it's not that difficult.

MASTING AND RIGGING SEQUENCE

As you did in Part II, read through the following steps to get an idea of how we'll proceed. The details for each step of the process will be covered more thoroughly later as we build the masts,

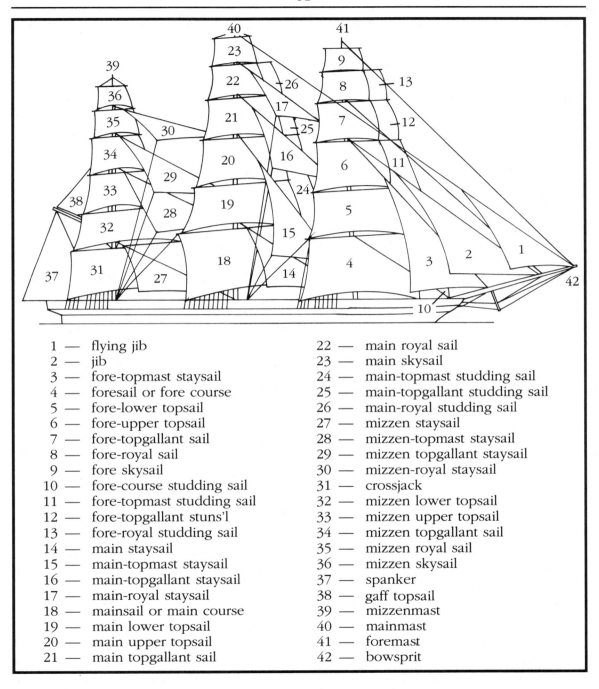

1 — flying jib
2 — jib
3 — fore-topmast staysail
4 — foresail or fore course
5 — fore-lower topsail
6 — fore-upper topsail
7 — fore-topgallant sail
8 — fore-royal sail
9 — fore skysail
10 — fore-course studding sail
11 — fore-topmast studding sail
12 — fore-topgallant stuns'l
13 — fore-royal studding sail
14 — main staysail
15 — main-topmast staysail
16 — main-topgallant staysail
17 — main-royal staysail
18 — mainsail or main course
19 — main lower topsail
20 — main upper topsail
21 — main topgallant sail

22 — main royal sail
23 — main skysail
24 — main-topmast studding sail
25 — main-topgallant studding sail
26 — main-royal studding sail
27 — mizzen staysail
28 — mizzen-topmast staysail
29 — mizzen topgallant staysail
30 — mizzen-royal staysail
31 — crossjack
32 — mizzen lower topsail
33 — mizzen upper topsail
34 — mizzen topgallant sail
35 — mizzen royal sail
36 — mizzen skysail
37 — spanker
38 — gaff topsail
39 — mizzenmast
40 — mainmast
41 — foremast
42 — bowsprit

FIGURE 32. *A fully rigged ship — lines and canvas galore.*

yards, booms and gaffs; add and rig their accessories; then rig everything to the hull. Here's what Part III will entail. We'll proceed as though we're modeling a full-rigged ship, on the theory that if you can rig a ship, you can rig a schooner or another sailing vessel:

Step 1: Assemble each mast (including tops) and the bowsprit.

Step 2: Taper and prepare the yards, booms, and gaffs.

Step 3: Fit the masts with all their blocks.

Step 4: Fasten futtock shrouds to the masttops.

Step 5: Rig the lower shrouds to the mast and let their ends hang until later.

Step 6: Rig the topmast shrouds to the deadeyes on the masttop and fit the ratlines to them.

Step 7: Fit the yards with the blocks, the footropes, the jackstays, and all the other accessories needed. Put the yards on the masts and rig the halyards and the yard lifts. Do the same for the gaffs and booms.

Step 8: Bend the sails to the yard.

Step 9: Step the masts through the deck.

Step 10: Rig the bowsprit's standing rigging, then step the bowsprit.

Step 11: Belay all running rigging to its respective pins in this sequence: yard lifts, halyards, sails.

Step 12: Connect standing rigging in this sequence: Foremast stays to the bowsprit; all the mizzenmast gaffs and boom rigging; mainmast center stays to the foremast; and finally, the mizzenmast center stays to the mainmast. By following the above sequence, the forestay and mainstay will have less chance to bend the masts and can be set up tightly in place. (If you're building a schooner, you'll have no mizzenmast; thus you'll have no mizzen stays, etc.) Do not cut the loose ends of the stays after you've tied them down; if a stay becomes slack during the rigging of the braces you can adjust it before gluing and cutting the loose end.

Step 13: Belay the yard lifts and halyards.

Step 14: Reeve the lower shrouds through the lower deadeyes.

Step 15: Rig the backstays to their deadeyes on all masts.

Step 16: Fit and belay all yard braces.

Step 17: Have a party!

BUILDING MASTS

If you think about it, the nautical tongue did not evolve randomly. Let's first run through a little terminology. Ships, barks, barkentines, (and, naturally, three-masted schooners) had three masts; schooners, ketches and yawls had two. The mast farthest forward is the *foremast;* the *mainmast* is just that, the largest; and the mast farthest aft is the *mizzen.*

The quest for speed and power over the years led to larger sails and more of them — and thus to higher masts. To the *lower mast* was added a second section that, naturally, became known as the *top-mast*. But as ships grew larger, the topmast itself was topped, with a *topgallant*. The process continued when the topgallant was extended with a *royal* mast, which was further topped with a *skysail* mast on some ships. These extensions took on the name of the masts on which they were located — the *mizzen royal mast*, the *fore topmast*. Sails and rigging take the name of the mast on which they sit: the *main topgallant yard* is on the main topgallant mast; the *mizzen topgallant yard* is on the mizzenmast; the *fore upper topsail* is on the foremast, etc.

BOWSPRITS. The bowsprit is actually a mast fitted almost horizontally at the bow of the ship. The bowsprit supported the *foremast stays* and carried the *jib* and *spritsails*. On early ships, the bowsprit consisted of one piece; later a *jibboom* was added to its end. Originally, these vessels carried a small flagstaff at the end of the bowsprit, but soon the flagstaff was replaced by a short mast called the *sprit topmast*, which supported a square sail called, not surprisingly, the sprit topmast sail. Another sail, the spritsail, was carried on the spritsail yard, which sits below the bowsprit. The *spritsail yard* was secured to the bottom of the bowsprit by a rope sling.

The sprit topmast was secured to the end of the bowsprit by a wooden knee mounted atop the bowsprit. The bottom of the sprit topmast was lashed to the end of the knee. Some vessels also had

a masttop and another mast over the lower one, just like the topmast on the other masts.

On some bowsprits, a pole called a martingale was attached to the underside of the jibboom cap by iron straps and was used to support the martingale stays. *Martingale stays* took the strain exerted on the jibboom by the jibs and the foremast stays. The jibboom carried the *foretopgallant stay* and the *foreroyal stay*. (These stays were called *inner jibstays* and *outer jibstays*, respectively.) On earlier ships of war, the martingale stays were secured to ringbolts under the bowsprit. Later, they were secured to ringbolts or plates on the side of the bow, as shown in Figure 33.

Bobstays counteracted the strain on the bowsprit exerted by the forestays. They were attached to ringbolts or plates just above the waterline on the stempost and rigged under the bowsprit by *deadeyes* and *lanyards*.

Assemble and rig the masts and bowsprit in a vise on your workbench before you glue them to the model. Before you even start, drill a number of different-sized holes in a foot-long piece of 2 X 4 to accommodate different-sized masts and yards. Group the yards together on their holder by their location on the masts so you don't mix them up. If you build them on your hull, you'll be forced to turn your model around everytime you need to turn the mast. This can get very touchy and irritating. Do it away from the model and there's less

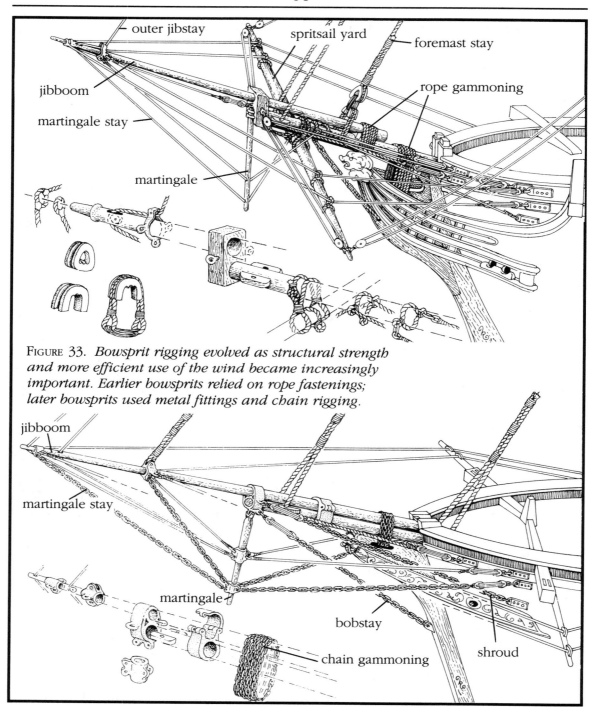

FIGURE 33. *Bowsprit rigging evolved as structural strength and more efficient use of the wind became increasingly important. Earlier bowsprits relied on rope fastenings; later bowsprits used metal fittings and chain rigging.*

chance of breaking something you labored over.

Now that we've got a rough idea of what we'll be working on, let's get to it. As with any construction work, the key to success lies in following a logical order that allows the builder to move on without backtracking or painting himself into a corner. Masting and rigging a model requires sticking to a sequence that will simplify the operation and let you avoid subtle rigging maneuvers in hard-to-reach spots — of which there are many.

Mast Parts

The masts support the yards, the sails, the booms and gaffs, and all the rigging needed to hold everything together and to move the sails to harness the wind. Kits will supply a number of pieces with which to construct your masts. Some parts may need painting or varnishing; check your plans and do this before you begin assembling the pieces.

TAPERING MASTS. Ship models use dowels for masts, and most kits supply them. Some dowels are walnut or some other dark wood; for models that require painted masts, kits will supply birch dowels. You'll still have to stain the upper masts, though, because on most ships this section was naturally finished with oil.

You'll likely run into some kind of problem with these dowels: Some are warped, some are precut and leave no

room on the ends to grip when you're tapering them, and some will be longer but require precise measuring to prevent waste — a difficult task at best. Chances are you'll have to buy extra dowels to get the job done properly.

Most masts are tapered toward the upper end; the sectional diameters are generally indicated in the plans. The best way to taper a mast is with a lathe. Unfortunately, a lathe is quite an expensive machine and, at least for beginners working on their first couple of models, too much of an investment. Don't worry, I've found something that works pretty well: a 1/4-inch or 3/8-inch electric hand drill, a bastard machinist's file followed by a smoother mill file, and then sandpaper.

If you have no lathe and don't want to fork over the money for a variable-speed drill (although for $30 to $40 such a drill is worth the investment), you must reduce the drill's speed. Otherwise you'll break the dowel and most likely hurt yourself. You can build a variable-speed outlet by using a household light dimmer (rheostat); but be careful not to run the drill at a reduced speed for more than 20 minutes at a time or you'll burn out its motor.

The first thing we want to do is reduce the size of the mast where it sets into the deck. This will also facilitate inserting the end into a drill chuck when we start to taper the mast; look at Figure 34. First determine the length of the mast to be reduced (check plans for the length

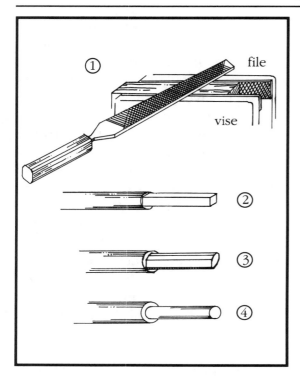

FIGURE 34. *Reducing the lower end of the mast.*

of the mast below deck) and mark it by cutting a line around the mast with an X-Acto saw. Set the mast in a vise and file it flat **(1)**. Next, turn the mast 90 degrees and set it in the vise with the flat side against one of the vise jaws. Flatten the second side and repeat this process until all four sides have been squared **(2)**. Next file the corners, one at a time, until you reach the diameter needed **(3 & 4)**. As you work, check for proper fit against holes in the deck. Now you can insert the reduced portion of the

mast in your drill or lathe and taper the other end as needed.

Set the mast in the drill chuck. (Even if the mast fits in the drill chuck without reduction, I prefer to reduce the lower end of every mast so I won't have to drill big holes in the deck planking.) Turn on the drill, and run a file across the mast's upper part while steadying the drill and the mast butt with your other hand. Use a glove so that the friction does not burn your fingers. The plans will indicate, for example, that the mast is 10 mm at the deck and 8 mm at its top. Measure the mast's diameter with a caliper while you reduce it. As you approach the proper diameter, switch to your smoother file. Once the proper taper is obtained with the file, sand the rough surface with a sanding board (which you can make by gluing a piece of fine sandpaper onto a paint mixing stick).

After the mast is tapered and sanded, you're ready to shape its upper part. If your model requires masts with the upper portions squared off, proceed as you did when you reduced the lower part to fit the deck hole, just don't round off the corners.

THE LOWER MAST. The lower mast is the heaviest, and in most cases it was built by *woolding* it — lashing together longitudinal sections with either rope or iron hoops (depending on the era in which the ship was built), as you can see in Figure 35. Of course, the masts on your model need not be made in sections like

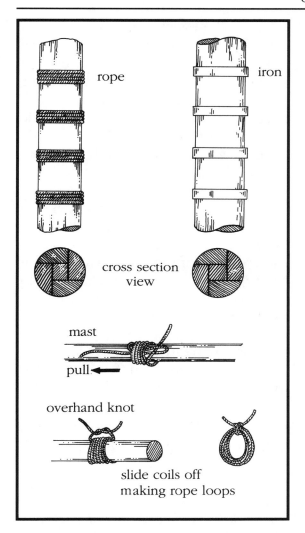

FIGURE 35. *Lower mast sections.*

for a number of other places on your model.

Make a small loop in some rigging line around the mast where you want the woolding and catch it with the fingernail of your left thumb (the opposite if you're lefthanded). Now coil the line two, three, or four times around the mast and over the loop. Then thread the free end of the line through the loop and pull the end of the loop until it is caught under the coils. Cut off any loose ends and add a dab of glue. You've got your woolding.

If you want to make rope loops to hang on a belaying pin rack, for example, use the same method — with two variations. Rather than the mast, wrap the line around the handle of an X-Acto knife clamped in a vise. When you've threaded the free end of the line through the loop and pulled it under the coil, tie an overhand knot in the two ends rather than cutting them off. Add a dab of glue and slip the loop off the knife handle. Now you've got a rope coil to hang on the belaying pin rack.

You can make iron hoops by using flat finish tape, black paper strips glued in place, or copper sheeting strips soldered into position. Be careful and clean. Some masts, for instance, are painted white before the hoops are fitted; if you use copper sheeting, the spot where you solder may burn the paint.

CHEEKS. The upper end of the lower mast supports the masttop. This structure

the real ones, so the hoops will be for authenticity rather than for strength.

The bottom part of Figure 35 shows the best way I know to make rope loops: You can use the loops as wooldings on the mast or — with variations — loops

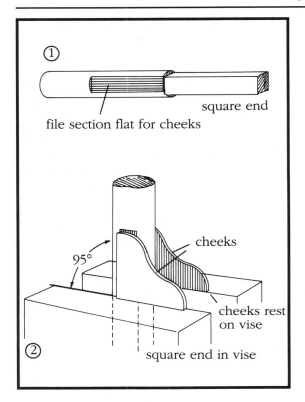

① file section flat for cheeks

square end

95°

cheeks

cheeks rest on vise

② square end in vise

FIGURE 36. *Preparing the mast for cheek installation.*

edges of the cheeks resting on the vise jaws **(2)**. If the mast is set at an angle (raked) on your model, make sure you set the mast in the vise at the same angle. This will allow the tops of the cheeks to remain parallel to the deck. For example, if the rake of the mast is 5 degrees, the angle between the back of the mast and the vise jaws will be 95 degrees.

MASTTOPS. On top of the cheeks are set two timbers — one on each side of the mast running fore and aft — called *trestletrees*. Running athwartships and resting on the trestletrees are the *crosstrees* (two or more, depending on the type of ship). Finally, on top of the crosstrees and trestletrees, planks form the floor of the top.

There are many different types of masttops but, except for the ones on steel masts, all are built with crosstrees and trestletrees. Most kit plans have drawings of masttops and they are generally clear

is supported by two shoulders, or cheeks, pegged to each side of the mast. (Most masts are cut square from the upper edge of the cheeks to the masthead. If your mast has a belaying pin ring, or a boom-supporting ring and brass sail hoops, insert it before setting the cheeks in place. Figure 36 shows how to ready a mast for the cheeks. First, file part of the upper section of the mast on each side to provide a flat surface for gluing the cheeks **(1)**. Insert the squared end of the mast in the vise with the flattened top

FIGURE 37. *Masts were a study in strength and utility. The lowest — and thickest — mast often was constructed from longitudinal sections banded together. At its top sat an assembly of crosstrees and trestletrees supported by cheeks; this assembly was often planked over to provide a working platform. Moving up the mast you'd find two more sections: the topmast (not the highest section as one would think), and then the topgallant. A mastcap held these two higher sections together and helped support the top crosstrees assembly.*

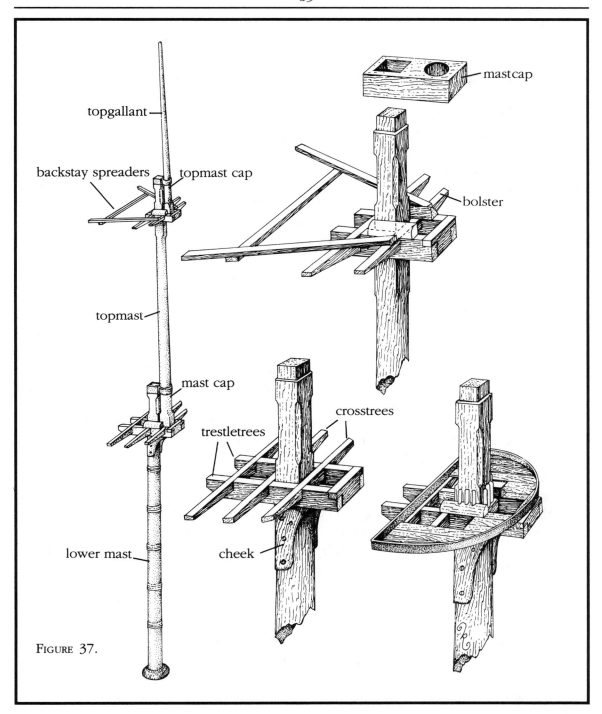

topgallant

backstay spreaders — topmast cap

mastcap

bolster

topmast

mast cap

crosstrees

trestletrees

lower mast

cheek

FIGURE 37.

MASTING AND RIGGING

enough to understand. Some kits even supply precut trestletrees and crosstrees, so all you have to do is fit them and glue them together. Some precut pieces are not satisfactory because (and I've never understood why) they are cut cross-grain and break at the slightest touch. I never use cross-grained, precut pieces; I make my own from hardwood such as maple or boxwood and I suggest you do the same.

Crosstrees and trestletrees are notched together so their top edges are flush. Figure 37 will give you an idea how they work. The trestletrees are set and glued on top of the cheeks and against the sides of the mast. The spacing of the crosstrees, which run perpendicular to the trestletrees, depends on the model you're building.

To cut the notches on the trestletrees, insert the two pieces together in a vise (Figure 38); mark with a pencil where the slots are and extend a line to indicate the depth of the cuts. Make sure the two trestletrees are perfectly even and the line for the depth of cut is flush with the edge of the vise jaws. Using an X-Acto saw, cut down on the lines marked for the slots; then break the piece off by gently twisting the saw blade sideways. If the slots are slightly uneven use a small file to clean the cuts. Repeat the process for the crosstrees.

Match the different pieces together to check that they fit properly and that they are flush on the upper side, where the planking will be applied. Then ap-

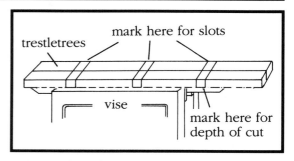

FIGURE 38. *Precision cutting is vital when aligning crosstrees and trestletrees; a vise helps.*

ply some glue in the slots and press the pieces together.

Another part of the top's framing consists of *bolsters*, wood blocks rounded on one side to provide a smooth surface on which the shrouds can rest (see Figure 37). You can make bolsters by filing one corner of a square piece of stock, or you can buy quarter-round molding in a hobby shop.

It's most important to ensure that everything is perfectly flat and that no distortions occur while the glue is drying. To do this, sandwich the entire structure between two pieces of scrapwood and clamp the whole thing together until the glue dries.

MASTTOP PLANKING. The framework of crosstrees and trestletrees was covered with planking to provide a working platform. The top's platform changed over time from the original round shape on early vessels to a rectangular and later

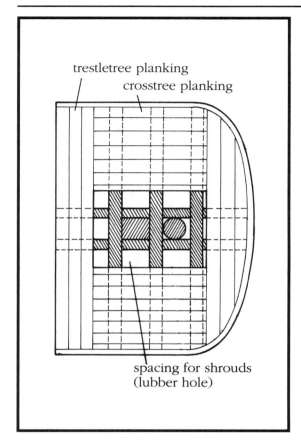

FIGURE 39. *Planking the masttop.*

the planking in a crosshatch pattern as shown in Figure 39. Some planks are set across crosstrees, while other planks are set across the trestletrees. Remember to leave a space on each side of the mast for the passage of the shrouds. Your plans will show where. After planking, glue a thin wood strip (0.5 mm by 3 mm) around the platform edge to finish the work nicely.

MASTCAPS. Just above the masttop you'll find the *mastcap* — a collar that held two mast sections together when one was erected at the head of the other, as in Figure 37. While mastcaps will vary in shape, material (wood, iron, steel), and size depending on the era, they all have two holes through which the two mast sections must pass (Figure 40). Most kits will supply precut or precast mastcaps; you can also buy mastcaps from suppliers. Here are a few types you may find in your kit: one wooden piece (**1**); two pieces held together by an iron band (**2**); wood in the shape of a boot (**3**); or two iron hoops welded together (**4**).

You'll find some problems with mastcaps. Often the holes cut in the caps are too small to accommodate the masts; gently enlarge the holes with a round file. On most of the flat, wooden caps, the hole for the lower mast is square — which is fine since we squared off the lower mast for the cheeks. When inserting the topmast through the cap, (which you should not do before the topgallant mast, if present, is rigged as described

almost triangular shape. Most kits provide precut plywood in the shape you need. The precut pieces will have to be planked over to simulate the real platforms.

If you're using a precut plywood platform, it's a good idea to plank after gluing the plywood piece to the framing. I normally glue the platform to the framing and clamp the assembly together until it is dry to prevent distortions. Apply

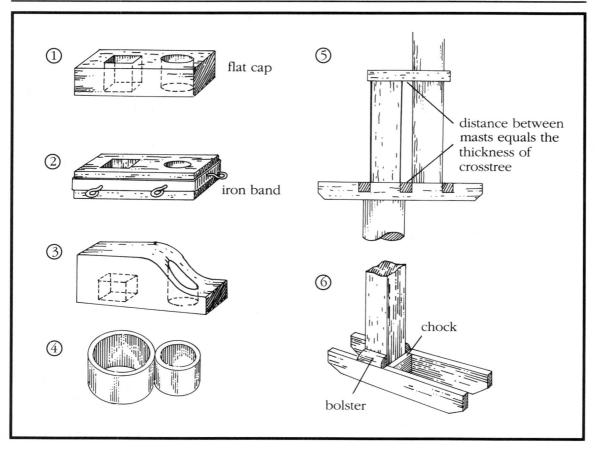

FIGURE 40. *Mastcap components.*

below) keep it in line with the lower mast. The distance between the two holes **(5)** should be equal to the space between the two masts at the top level. Normally this distance is equal to the thickness of the crosstree. If the type of top you're making does not have a crosstree in that location, you'll have to insert a wood spacer, called a *chock* **(6)**; note also the bolster.

CROSSTREES. Moving up the mast we come to an arrangement similar to the masttop, but now called the crosstrees, which connects the upper portion of the topmast to the lower part of the topgallant mast. Here the frame is not covered with planks. Since the upper side of the timbers does not need to be flush, the notches can be cut smaller to give the crosstrees more strength, as shown in

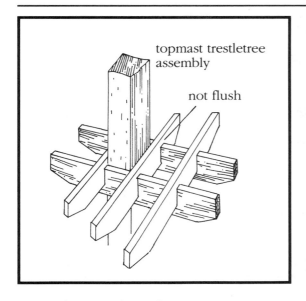

FIGURE 41. *Finishing the mast.*

PHOTO 23. *The masttop of a schooner. Notice the small rings below the deadeyes at the
ends of the crosstrees. The futtock shrouds will
be tied to these rings after the main shrouds
are rigged.*

Figure 41. Drill a hole into the ends of
the crosstrees to take the futtock shrouds,
according to your plans.

Fit the cap on the topgallant mast.
Then join the topgallant to the topmast,
making sure the two are aligned. Use
carpenter's glue on all parts, along with
a very small dab of ACC to hold them
together.

Next, affix the topmast and topgallant assembly to the lower mast. While
gluing these two components together,
check that the crosstrees are aligned with
the top. Also make sure that the whole
assembly is straight. The mast is now
ready to be furbished with blocks and
eyebolts.

Set the mast aside until later.

YARDS

Yards are spars suspended horizontally
from the masts to stretch the sails to the
wind. Figure 42 shows yards and how
to taper them.

The yards on early ships (17th and
18th century) had a thick octagonal
center portion and were rounded and
tapered toward the ends. The thicker
section provided a better gripping surface for *slings* and *jeers* — which held

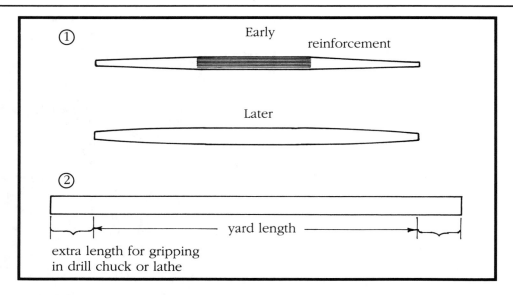

FIGURE 42. *Tapering yards.*

the yards to the masts and allowed them to be adjusted to the wind. In later ships, as the methods to secure and move the yards improved, the middle portion was rounded like the rest of the yard, and the tapering ran almost from the middle to the ends **(1)**.

Most kits supply a number of dowels (birch, walnut, lemonwood, etc.) from which to make the yards. The yards often must be cut from dowels of varying lengths. Just as with the masts, you'll often run short and have to buy extras.

TAPERING YARDS. As with the masts, the process of tapering is made a lot easier with a lathe. But if you don't have one, and there's really no reason for you to rush out and get one, you can still do

a good job of tapering. The trick is to cut the dowel longer than you need **(2)**, leaving a portion on each end to grip in a vise, lathe, or a drill chuck.

One way to taper the yards is to use your variable-speed electric drill or your current-reduction rheostat (again, no more than 20 minutes with this or you'll burn out your drill's motor), and the bastard machinist's file and the smoother mill file for finishing. Just leave the extra length at one end to fit into the drill chuck and sand away. When you're done, cut off the extra amount on each end.

If your yard is the earlier type with the unrounded, thicker middle, you can build this up by gluing eight strips about 0.5 mm thick around the yard, and then tapering their ends.

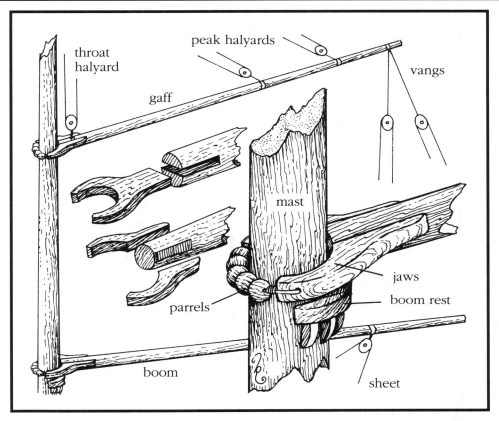

FIGURE 43. *Wind changes direction, hulls pitch and roll, and fore-and-aft sails must be raised and lowered. To allow the spars supporting these sails to rise, drop, and pivot while secured to the mast we have jaws, boom rests, and parrels.*

BOOMS AND GAFFS

Booms and *gaffs* take the place of yards for fore-and-aft rigged sails. On a schooner, booms and gaffs hold up the fore- and mainsails. On a square rigger a boom and a gaff support the foot and head (respectively) of the *spanker*, or *driver*. Unlike yards, they are often tapered only on one end. These spars are

secured to the mast by a fork-like extension called *jaws*, as shown in Figure 43. The jaws encircle the after half of the mast circumference and are secured around the forward half by a *parrel* — a rope inserted through round beads and tied at each end of the jaws.

The boom is supported at the mast by a wooden collar called a *boom rest*. This is glued to the mast and supported by small wooden brackets.

The jaws can be built and installed on the boom and the gaff in more than one way. One method is to cut the jaws from a piece of solid wood of the proper size and make a "throat" at the larger end so that it will fit halfway around the mast. This can be done either with a jigsaw or with a round file. Next, cut a slot on the boom end the size of the jaw piece and insert the jaw in it. Wind a small dark (to simulate tar) rigging line around the joint — a process called *serving* — to make the works more realistic.

Another method is to file a flat on either side of the boom or gaff end. Then cut two pieces of wood to the shape of half jaws and glue them to the flats. For realism you can drill two or three holes on each side and insert pins.

When rigging the gaff and boom parrels around the mast try this method: Tie an overhand knot on one end of the black rope and insert the rope in the hole at one side of the jaws. Next, insert the beads in the rope. To prevent the beads from rolling off, apply a little glue on the rope where the beads will stay. Next, set the jaws against the mast and thread the rope through the other hole in the jaws. Put a dab of fast-setting glue on the rope right on the spot where it will set in the hole; everything will stay taut.

Some ships built after around 1812, such as clippers, carried a *spencer mast* — a small-diameter mast that ran up the after side of the mizzenmast deck to masthead (Figure 44). It was secured at

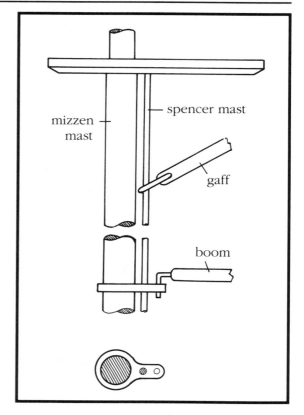

FIGURE 44. *The smaller spencer mast made it easier to attach gaffs.*

the top through a hole in the mizzen, in chocks between the trestletrees, or to an iron band around the mizzenmast. At the lower end it passed through a hole cut in a wooden collar which was secured to the mizzenmast and also served as a boom rest. The butt was then inserted into a hole in the deck. Some ships had spencer masts abaft the fore- and main-sails as well; these carried fore-and-aft rigged *spencer sails* similar to the spanker. The spencer masts provided a smaller spar for gaff jaws and hoops to have to encircle.

Rigging the spars

Here's a word of comfort — and one of caution — before we get started. Before we step the masts, we'll attach all the necessary rigging. That's going to create a temporary mess. Once you've rigged the masts and their fittings — the booms, the yards, the gaffs, and the sails — you'll have a lot of lines hanging down until you secure everything on the hull. If you separate the groups of lines and tape them together everything will become much simpler to identify. For example, tape the lower shrouds together at the bottom and they will not tangle with the rest of the lines.

Before we get into the actual rigging sequence, it's important to understand some terms vital to working with rope. When we talk about "securing and fitting the shrouds" or "rigging the mainstay," you'll be doing something involving the following:

To *belay* a line means secure it, in this context usually to a *belaying pin* on a bulwark.

To *reeve* a line is to lead it through a hole or a pattern of holes, in this context usually through deadeyes or sheaves.

To *seize* a line means permanently lashing two lines (or two parts of the

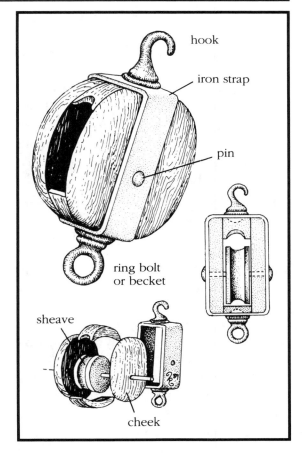

FIGURE 45. *Blocks, relatively simple mechanisms on which the entire movement of a ship rests.*

same line) together using *small stuff* — short lengths of smaller rope. When you fit a shroud to a mast you may wrap the shroud around the mast and then seize its end back on itself. Seizing is a complicated and exacting craft, especially on a model. And intricate seizing is not something at which a beginner should try his hand. We'll keep it simple: When I say "seize it," I mean use a simple overhand knot, a few wraps, and a dab of glue.

To *serve* a line means to wrap it tightly with small stuff to protect it from chafing.

Blocks and rigging line were small enough on life-size ships to accommodate human hands; when you're working in scale they become painfully tiny. In 1/8-inch scale a foot-long block is only 1/8-inch (or 3 mm) long. Even the thickest of shrouds becomes quite thin in scale. Blocks furnished with kits usually are out of scale; sometimes you'll get only one size. Choose your rigging line carefully, and make every effort to keep within scale: You can buy rigging line as small as 0.10 mm (.004 inch).

Standing rigging was tarred; use black line for that. Running rigging, which sailors handled, was not tarred; use cream or tan line for that.

RIGGING SEQUENCE

Step 1: Fit masts with blocks.
Step 2: Rig the futtock shrouds.
Step 3: Rig the lower shrouds.
Step 4: Rig the topmast shrouds.
Step 5: Rig the topgallant shrouds.
Step 6: Fit the ratlines to the upper shrouds (called "rattling down").
Step 7: Brush diluted glue over knots.
Step 8: Fit the yards with the blocks, the footropes, and the jackstays.
Step 9: Bend the sails (if you're using them) to the yards.

Step 10: Put the yards on the masts and rig the halyards and the yard lifts. Do the same for the gaffs and boom.
Step 11: Affix the booms, gaffs and spencer masts.
Step 12: Step the masts.
Step 13: Rig, fit, and step the bowsprit.

BLOCKS. The first step in rigging your model calls for attaching blocks to the various spars. The exact arrangement of blocks and eyebolts depends on the ship you're building. Take a look at the plans and determine:

• Whether you need holes in the masts for halyard sheaves, or whether the halyards are rove through blocks instead;
• Where you'll install the blocks for the yard lifts;
• Where, if you need them, you'll put the lower yard trusses and the lower topsail yard cranes;
• Where you'll install the cleats or supports for the yards' sling chains;
• Where you put the blocks for the peak and throat halyards for gaffs.

Makes it sound like you'll be looking for obscure parts for the rest of the day, doesn't it? It's really not as involved as it seems; just follow the plans.

Look for oval-shaped blocks made from hardwood such as maple, oak, or boxwood. It's possible to make your own blocks, but that's a process best reserved for later. If you're building a large-scale model, you can buy blocks that already have sheaves in them.

Blocks are made of shaped wooden pieces (see Figure 45) held together by a strap made of rope on earlier ships, metal on later ships. On some blocks (maybe as many as 50 percent) you'll find an iron ringbolt, or *becket*, riveted to the strap. On the other end of the strap is either a rope tail or an iron hook, depending on the era and the block's specific job. A *sheave* (a grooved insert on which the line will move — a pulley), held in place by an iron pin that goes through the cheeks and the iron strap, is inserted in the space between the two cheeks.

Blocks are made with one or more sheaves. With more sheaves the pulling load could be further reduced and fewer men were needed to accomplish a given task. *Halyards* (which raised and lowered some spars), were tied to the yard, passed over a sheave inserted in the mast, and run down to the bulwarks, where they were rigged to a purchase (Figure 46) made of two or more blocks having one or more sheaves. This reduced the pulling load considerably.

Deadeyes — round blocks with three holes drilled in a triangular pattern in their sides — secured the lower end of a shroud or stay to the ship. A deadeye on the end of a lower mainmast shroud, for example, could be connected to a deadeye on a chainplate by reeving a rope called a *lanyard* through the three holes in each of the deadeyes.

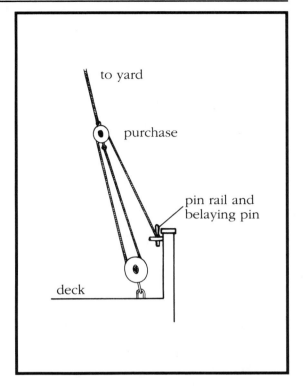

FIGURE 46. *Halyards run through blocks on deck; a blessing for seamen raising and lowering sails.*

There are different ways to secure blocks in place, as Figure 47 shows. To strap a block, use black annealed wire, #33 or #34, depending on the block size. This wire is best because it will not break when twisted with pliers, and it adds a very authentic look. As you strap it, furnish each block with a becket, the ring used to tie a line to a block. To make a becket just leave the wire slightly loose and push the end of an awl through it

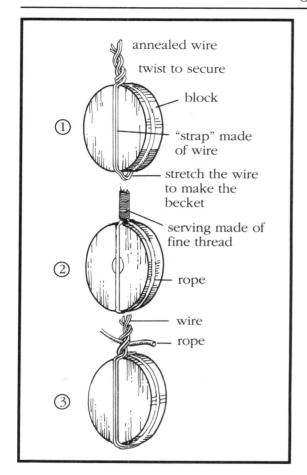

FIGURE 47. *Securing blocks.*

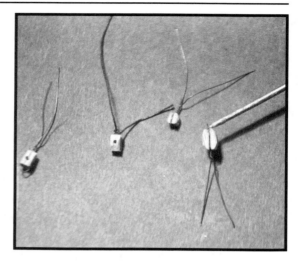

PHOTO 24. *Blocks rigged with wire. Notice the tip of the awl inserted in the block's becket.*

after the wire is twisted on the other end of the block **(1)**.

To attach a block to a line (such as a short rope tail or pendant on the end of a yard) you can either wrap the rope around the block and seize the end back on itself with fine thread **(2)**, or strap the block with wire, insert the rope between the wire ends, and twist the wire a few

more turns **(3)**. Then wrap the short end of the rope around the twisted part of the wire and the rope itself, and apply a dab of glue to it. Cut the excess wire.

Varnish all your blocks after you've installed them.

FUTTOCK SHROUDS. *Futtock shrouds,* if present, are short iron rods (or ropes on ships built prior to about 1820) that secure the topmast shrouds to the deadeyes. There are a number of ways they can be installed, as Figure 48 shows. Depending on the model you're constructing, the futtock shrouds will be secured either to an iron mastband or to a sheerpole tied to the lower shrouds. On some ships the topmast futtock shrouds were tied to lines that were

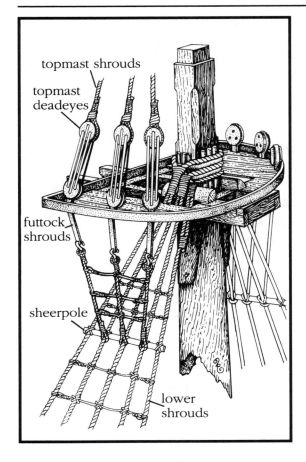

FIGURE 48. *Futtock shrouds, iron rods or rope shrouds through the masttop platform, countered the pull of the upper shrouds, adding stability and balance to the mast.*

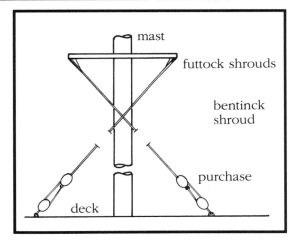

FIGURE 49. *Captain William Bentinck gave his name to this arrangement.*

rigged to opposite sides of the deck with purchases (Figure 49), an arrangement called a *bentinck* shroud (after Royal Navy Captain William Bentinck, its inventor).

If your model calls for sheerpoles or the cross-deck arrangement you won't be able to secure the futtock shrouds yet because the lower shrouds are not rigged and the mast is not installed on the model. Here's a simple solution: Twist a loop just below the masttop in the wire that forms the futtock below the top. This will keep the futtocks where you want them until you're ready to rig them. See Photo 23 on page 73

LOWER SHROUDS. The shrouds, whether lower, top, or topgallant, provided the mast with lateral support. On real ships, shrouds were usually installed in pairs, or *gangs*, to spread the pressure exerted on the mast. For your model, your plans will dictate the number and sequence with which they will be secured to the mast. The secret is making sure the ends of the shrouds are even at the channels. You can temporarily set the masts on the hull to get the shrouds'

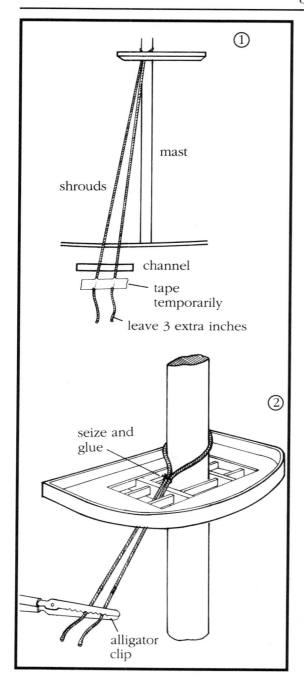

① mast

shrouds

channel

tape temporarily

leave 3 extra inches

② seize and glue

alligator clip

FIGURE 50. *Rigging lower shrouds.*

length. Cut all shrouds about 3 inches longer than the measured distance because you'll need the extra length when you tie them to the deadeyes before reeving the lanyards. See Figure 50. Run the shroud around the lower mast above the trestletrees and drop and tape both ends evenly **(1)** just below where they will attach to the channels when the masts are stepped. Figure 50 shows how the shrouds will look when the masts are placed on the hull. Take an alligator clip and place it on the shrouds just below the trestletrees — this will keep them from slipping. With a simple overhand knot in a short section of a separate piece of rigging line, tie the shrouds just above the trestletrees (see Figure 48 on page 81); apply a dab of glue **(2)**. Tape or clip the lower ends together until later. Alternate sides with each pair of shrouds.

TOPMAST AND TOPGALLANT SHROUDS. Apply the same method to the topmast shrouds. Run the shrouds around the topmast above the masthead crosstrees, clip, seize above the clip, glue the seizing knot.

The next step is to rig the lower ends of the topmast shrouds to the topmast deadeyes, if these are present; then you'll be able to install the topgallant shrouds. Here again, however, you will find different construction details from ship to ship. On some, the topmast shrouds are rigged via deadeyes through the tops to the futtock shrouds, as in Figure 48. On others (Figure 51), the shrouds pass through holes in the ends of the

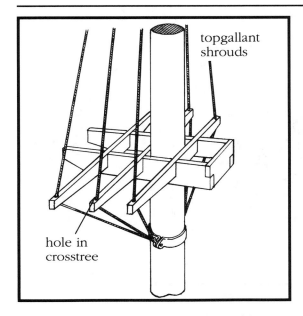

FIGURE 51. *Topmast deadeye assemblies.*

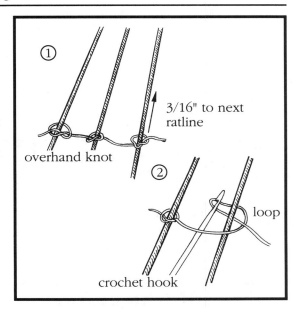

FIGURE 52. *Upper ratlines.*

crosstrees, becoming the futtocks, and are tied to a ring on the mast band; the deadeyes are dispensed with. In the latter case, belay the shrouds to the mast band. In the former case, once the topmast shrouds are seized to the deadeyes, it's time to reeve lanyards through the upper and lower deadeyes of each pair; a simple technique for this can be found under "An Easy Way," page 100.

This is the time to set up the topgallant shrouds, which will seem straightforward after the topmast shrouds.

RATLINES. Now is the time to rattle down the upper shrouds. Use an overhand knot to tie the *ratlines* — the rope ladders sailors use to climb the masts —

to the shrouds (see Figure 52). At model size, this knot looks better than the traditional clove hitch because it is simpler and neater **(1)**. Ratlines were not tarred, thus the rigging line you'll use for ratlines is cream-colored — and smaller than any other rigging line you'll use on the model. The vertical distance between the ratlines on a real ship was usually 16 inches, which works out to around 3/16 of an inch on a 1/8-inch scale model. I judge this distance by eye, but you can also slip a strip of wood between the lines for proper spacing. To turn the line around the shroud I first make a loop, then push the loop behind the shroud and catch it on the other side with a crochet hook **(2)**. Leave a short piece of

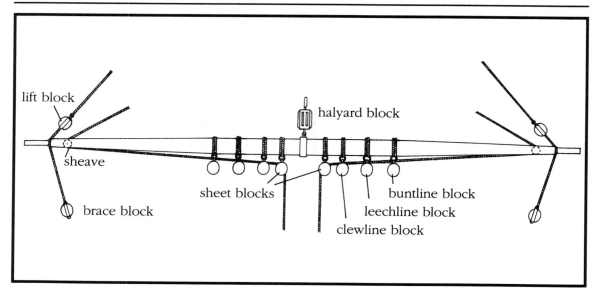

FIGURE 53. *Basic yard blocks.*

rigging line on the end knots to be cut later.

When you've rattled down the upper shrouds, paint everything with diluted carpenter's glue and let it dry. The glue will secure the knots and stiffen the whole assembly. Now cut the ratline ends with a very sharp pair of scissors. Once this is done your masts are ready for their yards.

YARDS — BASIC RIGGING

The yards are fitted with many gadgets to provide for their proper operation, including any number of blocks. The details will vary depending on the era and the type of vessel. Yards were also fitted with basic running tackle to lift and lower, orient, and support the yards on the masts. Figures 53 and 54 show the complexity of rigging yards. And that's not all — yards have a number of other accessories.

Now that the masts have been fitted with their blocks, the lower shrouds have been seized, and the upper shrouds have been rattled down, we can furbish the yards with yokes, parrels, or slings, as indicated in your plans.

Yards (topmast, topgallant, royal, etc.) that have no fixed yokes or trusses should be pinned to the masts to keep them from sliding up and down.

Figure 55 shows some accessories.

YARD BANDS. Iron bands with eyes were used on some vessels to secure the

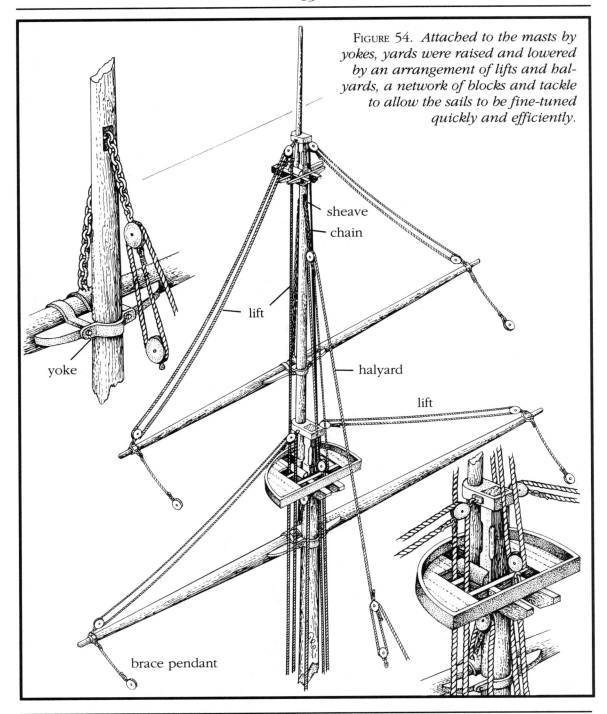

FIGURE 54. *Attached to the masts by yokes, yards were raised and lowered by an arrangement of lifts and halyards, a network of blocks and tackle to allow the sails to be fine-tuned quickly and efficiently.*

sheave

chain

lift

yoke

halyard

lift

brace pendant

blocks to the yard. Make yard bands with black paper or copper sheathing, with little eyebolts inserted through drilled holes **(1)**, or with ropes (thread) with small loops tied into them **(2)**. In small models, use the tails of the wires that strap the block to simulate the bands **(3)**. Pay close attention to your plans for the number, size, and location of every block on the yard.

A little calmness reminder: Make sure the blocks in your kit are the correct sizes before installing them. Chances are they won't be.

SHEAVES. Sheaves are inserted in a yard or a mast to provide a smooth passage for a rigging line **(4)**. To install a sheave, drill two or three holes as required to form a cut long and wide enough to receive the sheave. Cut across the holes until you obtain the space needed. Then drill a small hole across the cut and insert the sheave in the slot and pin in the hole to hold the sheave in place.

FOOTROPES. When sailors had to move out on the yards to tend the sails, they stepped on *footropes* suspended about three feet below the yards and supported by other ropes called *stirrups* **(5)**. If the yard carried stunsail booms additional footropes called *Flemish horses* were installed at its end.

Manuals and kit plans suggest a variety of methods for fitting footropes.

I've found that the following method works well for me: Use black rigging line for the stirrups and cream-colored line for the footropes. For the stirrups, tie a clove hitch around the yard **(6)** and secure the knot with a touch of glue. Cut off the upper end. Tie an overhand knot on the lower end of the line, insert the footrope in the overhand knot and secure it with a touch of glue. Make fast the ends of the footropes to the yards with a clove hitch.

JACKSTAYS. Sails were held to yards by lacing them to *jackstays* on the yards' upper sides. Until the early 19th century jackstays were made of rope laced through eyebolts screwed to the top of the yard. Later the rope was changed to an iron rod **(7)**. Jackstays served a second purpose — and one that preserved the life of more than one sailor aloft — a solid place to grip. For your model, either build up the jackstays from eyebolts and rope or wire, or use stamped jackstays, which you can buy from suppliers.

To install the jackstays, hold the yard in a vise and mark the spots for the eyebolts. Drill holes and glue the eyebolts. If your model requires a rope jackstay, thread some cream-colored rigging line through the eyebolts, applying a spot of glue to each of them. If your model requires an iron rod, use model airplane steel wire, threading it through the eyebolts and soldering the ends. The steel rod looks best painted black.

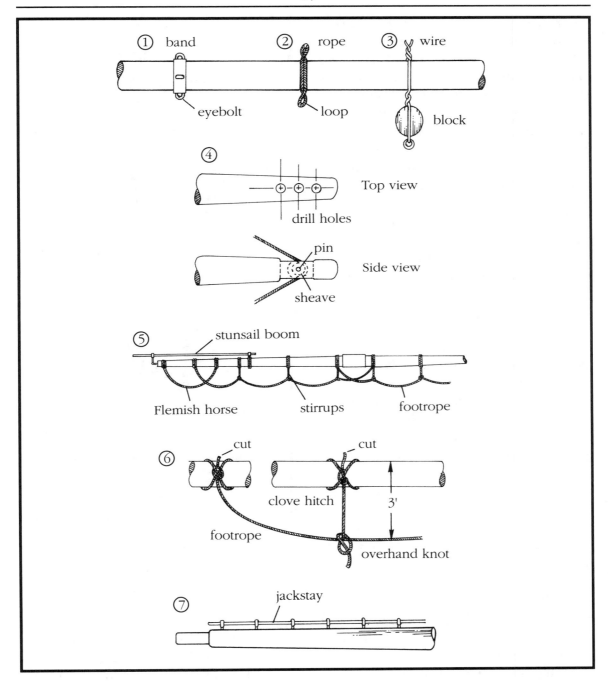

FIGURE 55. *Yard accessories.*

YOKES AND PARRELS. *Yokes* and *parrels* — arrangements of wood blocks, ribs, trucks (rollers), and ropes — were used to hold the upper yards to the masts and allow them to be raised or lowered as needed. If you don't find precut yokes in your kit, they are easy enough to make from a strip of scrapwood, using a round file the same size as the mast. Glue the yoke onto the yard, and drill a hole through the yard and the yoke. Set a pin in the hole and push the pin into the mast. This will hold the yard in place while you install the band. All three bands (Figure 56) can be made of copper sheeting or black tape **(1)**, although another easy way to simulate the mast band is to drill two holes in the yokes and run a piece of black wire through them and around the mast **(2)**.

On ships built before the 19th century, the upper yards were secured to the mast by *parrels* **(3)**. Parrels were made with wooden ribs, each rib receiving two holes for the passage of ropes.

A very simple way to simulate a yard parrel is shown in **(4)**. Turn some black thread around the mast and the yard in a square lashing, ending with an overhand knot in the back of the mast. Repeat the turns two or three times if you like.

Rollers (also called *trucks*) were set between the parrel's ribs by passing the ropes through the rollers and then lashing the rope around the yard. This system allowed the yard to be raised or lowered quite easily. If you wish, you can

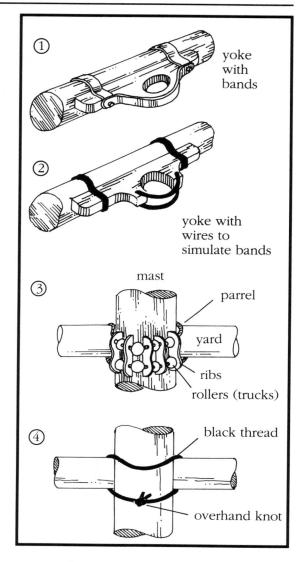

FIGURE 56. *Yokes and parrels.*

approximate this configuration with the method of stringing parrel beads (or trucks) described earlier in booms and gaffs.

TRUSSES, SLINGS, AND JEERS. A number of methods were developed to hold the lower yards in place and allow them to be adjusted to the wind, as shown in Figure 57. *Trusses* allowed the lower yards to be adjusted laterally. On older ships, trusses were made of rope turned around the mast **(1)** and the yard and brought down to the deck, where they were secured with a *purchase* — tackle arranged to mechanically increase the force a sailor could apply. Later trusses were made of iron. An iron band with a swivel joint holding the yard was secured around the mast **(2)**. This allowed the yard to be oriented to the wind as needed.

The weight of the yard was supported by a *sling*. Before the 19th century, the sling was made of heavy rope turned over the mastcap, fed through the masttop and tied to the center of the yard **(3)**. Later, a chain was used instead, and it was turned over a cleat behind the mast and fitted to an iron band on the middle of the yard **(4)**.

On older vessels, *jeers* also were used to raise or lower the yards for repairs as needed. Jeers were lines hung to the mast on a rope sling supported on each side by wooden cleats. A double block hung on the end of the sling and another double block was seized to the yard. The fall of this tackle was then brought to the deck, where it was rigged to another purchase and secured to belaying pin racks. The jeers were set in pairs, one on each side of the mast **(5)**.

STUNSAIL BOOMS. *Stunsails* were small sails carried by some ships on the ends of their yards to aid light-air performance. These sails were held by stunsail booms that extended the length of the yards, as we see in Figure 58.

Stunsail booms were supported by two iron rings. The inside ring wrapped around the boom and was fixed to a short iron rod that ran to another ring secured to the yard. The one on the end of the yard was supported by a bent iron rod inserted into the yard end. These rings are sometimes supplied in the kits, but if not, you can make your own. Here are some simple ways to make them. For the one at the end, use brass wire. Bend it over the tip of a pair of roundnose pliers or over a dowel of the right size to form the ring, and then bend the wire. You can also cut the ring from brass tubing and solder it to a brass wire.

The inside iron can be made in different ways. One way is to cut two rings from brass tubing and solder them together. Another is to flatten a piece of brass wire with a hammer, shape it into two rings and then solder them together. Still another way is to use #32 black annealed wire and bend it over the yard and the stunsail boom in a figure-eight fashion (two or more turns) and then twist the ends below the yard.

LIFTS. *Lifts* are tackles that support the weight of the ends of the yards and hold them horizontal. On earlier ships the lifts were combined with sheets (lines

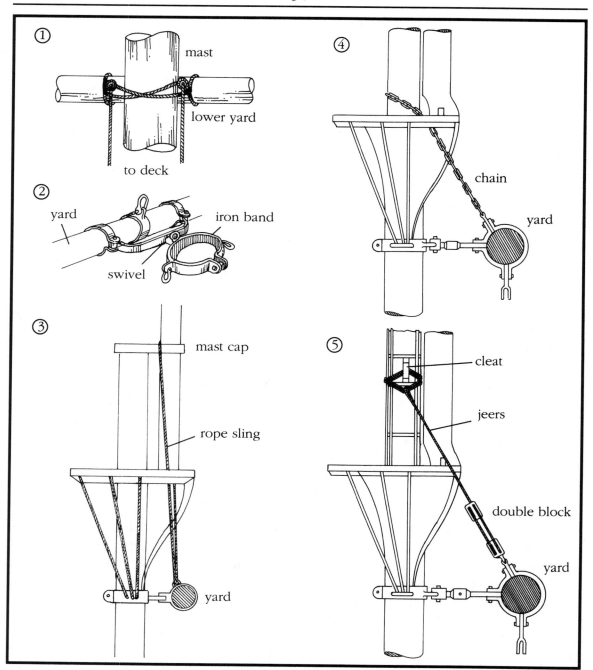

FIGURE 57. *Trusses, slings, and jeers.*

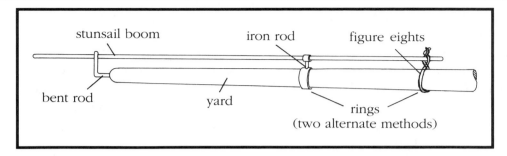

FIGURE 58. *Stunsail booms.*

used to trim the sails) and rove through blocks and tackles from the ends of the yards to the mastcaps and down to the deck. After about the end of the 18th century the lifts were rigged on their own so that no blocks were used and a single line ran from the mastcap to the end of the yard. The important fact is that every ship carrying yards will have lifts, so you must look for them on your plans and install them as indicated.

HALYARDS. *Halyards* are tackles for hoisting and lowering the upper yards along the masts (a function taken over by jeers or slings on the heavy lower yards). The yards were dropped to their lowest position to ease sail furling. (So if you build a model with no sails or furled sails, remember to lower the yards.) The halyards themselves varied according to the yards on which they were used.

On large warships the topsail yards carried a halyard passing through double blocks on each side of the mast. The topgallant and royal yards had either block and rope tackles, or a sheave inserted in the masthead with a rope or a chain running from an iron band on the yard up through the sheave and then down to a purchase on deck. After the introduction of the double topsail, the halyards on the upper topsail were run to an iron block and led down to a purchase on deck.

You will find the precise arrangements in your plans, but bear in mind that every yard will have a halyard, sling, or jeers that must be installed at this stage of construction.

The ends of your lifts and halyards should be left loose until you are ready to belay them to the pins — that is, after the masts are installed in the model.

BRACES AND PENDANTS. *Braces* are tackles that trim the yards into or off the wind. On warships, the blocks were attached directly to the band on the end of the yard, but on merchant vessels, the blocks dangled from the yards on ropes or chains called *pendants*. Get the yards ready for the braces by attaching the blocks now. To ease the final rigging process, the braces themselves won't be rigged until we've stepped the masts. (See page 106.)

Gaff rigging. The gaff rigging consists of a *throat halyard* and a *peak halyard*. The throat halyard lifts or lowers the gaff along the mast and consists of two blocks (single, double, or triple depending on the size of the gaff) — one secured to the jaws and the other under the masttop. The fall from this tackle is belayed on the fife rail.

The peak halyard supports the end of the gaff and the sail. This halyard often is rove through two single blocks seized on top of the gaff at a set distance from each other and two more single blocks secured on the mast above the masttop. The end of the gaff is always peaked up to follow the cut of the upper edge of the sail. The gaff is lowered when the sails are furled on the boom. The gaff is controlled from the deck by *vangs* — lines rove through a pair of double blocks attached by pendants to the tip of the gaff and belayed to a cleat on each bulwark. Vangs kept the gaff from sagging off to leeward.

Boom rigging. The boom is supported on its after end by the *topping lift*. An eyebolt is secured by an iron band to the boom. A rope pendant runs from the eyebolt to a block about halfway toward the masttop. The topping lift rigging starts at the becket of a block secured to an eyebolt just below the masttop; it reeves through the block on the pendant, back through the block at the masttop, then down to belay on the pinrail.

Bowsprit rigging. Think of a bowsprit as nothing more than a mast that's leaning forward. Take a look at Figure 33 on page 64 to see the variations in bowsprit rigging. As with the masts, rig and fit your bowsprit on the workbench, not the hull.

Like the lower mast, the bowsprit is hooped. Up until about the mid-19th century a *gammon lashing* held it to the stempost of the ship. Later the rope gammoning was replaced with iron or chain.

The jibboom is fixed to the bowsprit by a cap and gammoning. Depending on the era of your model the jibboom stays were either rope or chain. *Bobstays* — which counteracted the lift of the forestay — were originally heavy rope, evolving into chains or iron bands. Likewise for *martingale stays* — which counteracted the lift of the headstays.

The spritsail yard was secured to the bottom of the bowsprit by a rope sling. Fit eyebolts on the upper side of this yard through which to reeve the spritsail stays. Later, these stays can be fixed to the deadeyes outboard of the bow.

Like any other yard, the spritsail yard will require lifts and braces — it may also

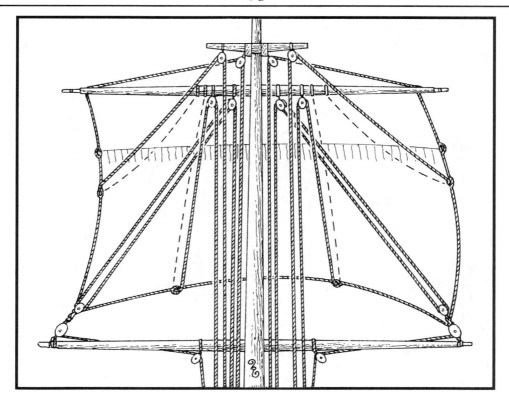

FIGURE 59. *Yards were given a multitude of fittings to accommodate the spider's web of rigging needed to raise or lower sails. Why display full sails on your model after all the work of rigging the yards?*

need a halyard. Check the plans. The final phase before the bowsprit is stepped calls for afixing any mast bands or eyebolts to secure the standing rigging.

THE SAILS

It's reminder time. If you plan to put sails on your model, do it before you step the masts; it will help you avoid a lot of problems.

Before I get too carried away, let me say that some ship models look good with sails. A fishing schooner looks great.

On the other hand, a lot can be said about sails on models, and not much of it is good. Why bother to spend hour upon hour painstakingly rigging your model and then cover everything with sails? Doesn't make much sense to me.

PHOTO 25. *Sails are rigged to the yards with a running stitch — a relatively simple operation. Notice how a furled sail can help you show off your rigging.*

It's quite impossible to find fabric that is thin enough to be in scale with your model; even if you could it would be next to impossible to sew it with a sewing machine.

Not to belabor the point, but here's another thing: To be installed properly, sails require a lot more rigging lines. All these extra lines must be belayed on belaying pin racks that are already bristling with belaying pins. Each sail will need sheets, buntlines, leechlines, and clewlines: that's eight lines going to the belaying pin racks. If you are rigging a clipper ship every mast will carry five sails; you'll need at least 40 extra belaying pins on the racks. In such a small scale, that's impossible.

The sails take their name from the yard or the stay to which they are rigged. You may find a *lower main staysail* or a *topgallant sail* as well as *stunsail, jibboom staysail,* and a *spritsail.* You could find as many as 38 pieces of canvas (sails) on a clipper ship. Lots of fun — if you like to sew!

Consider Figure 60. Some kits include sheets of material for the sails — some trace the contour of the sails on the fabric while others print the stitch-

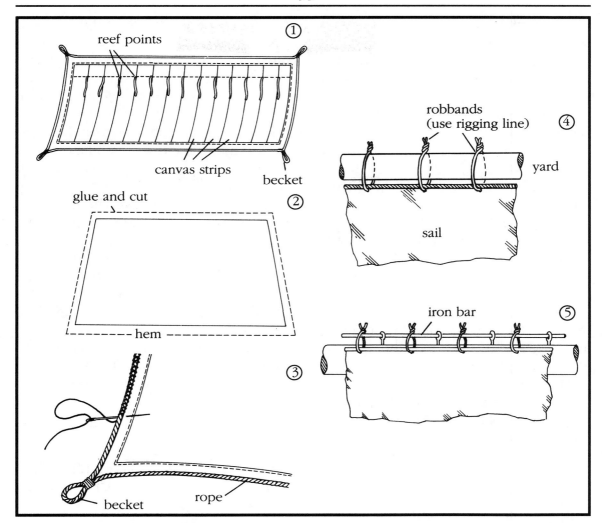

FIGURE 60. *Making sails.*

ing across to simulate the seams of the strips of canvas of which the sail was made.

To create good model sails — and as close to scale as possible — you'll have to create some, if not all, of the following effects: double-stitched seams, hemmed edges reinforced with rope (the boltropes), looped corners with metal inserts, rows of reef points **(1)**. You'll have to do this with a sewing machine and a standard sewing needle. If your kit contains prestamped sails, you may want to leave the canvas stitching on the print and save a lot of work. You must be able to sew perfect lines on a sewing machine to accomplish this task, or you must ask somebody to do it for you. Me? I can't do it.

The edges of sails must be hemmed to prevent fraying. It's a good idea to wet the cloth (where you cut it) with a brush and a bit of diluted carpenter's glue. The hemming is very difficult and should be done by someone who knows their way around a sewing machine **(2)**.

The next step is to sew a thin rope around the edges of the sail. With a sewing needle and very fine sewing thread put a running stitch over the rope and through the edge of the sail **(3)**. Make a small loop with the rope at the corners of the sail to form the beckets.

The sails are attached to the yard by ropes called robbands. On the early ships the robbands were laced around the yard **(4)** or, later, to either rope or iron jack-stays **(5)**.

Reef points, short tapered lengths of cord sewn through the sail in rows, allowed the sail's area to be reduced as the wind's speed increased by pulling in (reefing) the sails and tying the reef points to the yard. Some lower sails held as many as four rows of reef points, some — such as a topgallant — had none. Such sails would be furled long before the wind blew hard enough to require reefing the lowers. Check your plans.

Here's an easy method to install reef points: Run a stitch across the sail with your sewing machine. Thread a needle and tie a knot about one inch from the end of the thread. Insert the needle on the stitched line on the sail; apply a bit of glue to the knot and pull it through the sail. Now cut the thread on the other side of the sail and you will have a reef point. If you like, do the same thing without using a knot on the thread. Starch the sails or leave them floppy; stain the sails in light tea or leave them natural.

If you like the sails furled, make sure you use the thinnest material you can find or they will look too clumsy. Also make sure you tie the robbands in place for a more authentic look.

If you must install the sails, try to install them half-furled. This at least will allow some of the rigging to be shown.

STEPPING THE MASTS AND BOWSPRIT

Things are really coming together now and we're ready for the next phase — stepping the masts. We've completed the masts, the yards, the bowsprit, the running rigging such as yard lifts, halyards, and brace pendants; we've installed the upper shrouds and rattled them down, we've bent on the lower shrouds and left them hanging, to be rigged and rattled down later. All this preparation will make

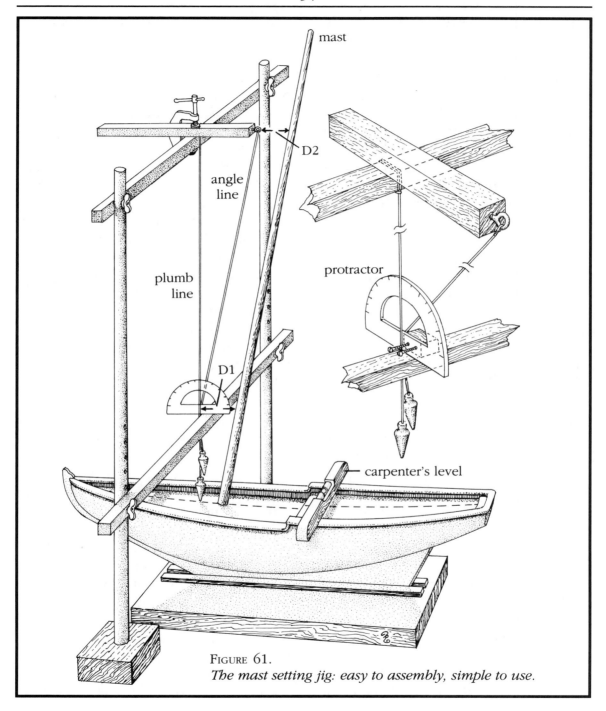

mast

D2

angle
line

plumb
line

protractor

D1

carpenter's level

FIGURE 61.
The mast setting jig: easy to assembly, simple to use.

it a lot easier to belay everything to the hull because you won't be working in tight and awkward positions.

As we talked about earlier in Part III (seems like a long time ago doesn't it?), I reduce the part of the masts that will be inserted through the holes in the deck (to 1/4-inch or 6 mm diameter) when making the lower masts. This makes it easier to drill the holes in the deck and reduces the chance of splintering the deck planking.

The most important part of this installation is to make sure that the mast assemblies are set square athwartships and raked to the proper angles fore and aft. The rake of each mast is always indicated in your plans.

Mast Stepping Jig

To do this properly I've developed a simple jig that's very easy to build. Take a look at Figure 61. Basically the assembly is not unlike a football goalpost, only with two crossbars and a few other differences. You'll be able to slip your hull underneath and set the rake of your masts with ease.

For the base, cut two 6-inch pieces from a 2 X 4 and drill 1/2-inch holes in the middle of each block. For the uprights, use 1/2-inch dowels about two feet long. You'll need six holes in each, about a half-inch apart. Place the uprights side by side on the workbench with ends flush, mark where the holes will sit, then put them in a vise and drill them. Be

careful here. The holes should be at identical heights in each upright, and be wide enough to fit a 1/8-inch machine bolt. Insert the uprights in the 1/2-inch holes in the 2 X 4 blocks. The jig needs one crossbar that you can move up and down to accommodate various heights of models.

For the movable crossbar, we'll use a 3/4-inch by 3/4-inch square piece of pine, about a foot long. Drill a hole in each end of the bar, leaving a half-inch or so at each end. Do the same for the upper crossbar. Now connect the lower and upper crossbars with the uprights.

Next, take a third 3/4-inch square strip of pine, about a foot or so long, and screw in an eyebolt (or drive in a nail) in one end. Clamp this strip at right angles to the upper crossbar; we'll be adjusting it later. Let's call this the gallows beam.

Next grab a protractor, some black thread, and a sinker from your fishing gear.

Here's how it works: Tie the sinker on the end of the thread and wrap the thread around the middle of the upper crossbar. Secure it temporarily with a simple knot so you can adjust it later; this will be your plumb line. Tie a second line on the eyebolt at the end of the gallows beam. Set your model on a flat surface (the keel board, preferably) and put a carpenter's level across the bulwarks. Level your model and set it aside for the moment; set the lower crossbar so that it's about 4 inches higher than the model. Set the protractor on the lower crossbar next to the plumb line so that the vertical zero line is exactly in line with the plumb line.

Glue a small block of wood to the protractor and use a clothespin to hold the protractor assembly in place on the lower crossbar. Adjust the gallows beam so that it's directly above the eyebolt holding the plumb line. This will represent a mast at 90 degrees. Next, take the string on the end of the gallows beam and set it on the lower crossbar at the same point where the plumb line crosses the lower crossbar. The two strings should meet at the centerline on the protractor.

As you slide the gallows beam forward or backward, the string on its end will move along the arc of the protractor. Get the angle of rake from your plans, slide the gallows beam until the string matches that angle on the protractor, and clamp it down.

Here's another tip before we get started: If you set the mizzenmast first, the mainmast second, and the foremast last, it will be easier to remove the jig from the model. Let's get started.

STEPPING THE MAST. Remove the protractor. Straddle the model with the jig so that the sinker on the end of the plumb line is centered in front of the mast hole. Insert the mast in the hole and align it with the plumb line, looking from aft of the model. Next, move to the side of the model and adjust the mast to match the angle we just set with the second string.

"How do you do that?" you ask. The distance (D1) from the mast to the point where the two lines rest against the lower crossbar should be equal to the distance (D2) from the knot on the eyebolt on the upper strip to the mast. After you've made a dry run, dab some glue on the bottom of the mast and insert it at the proper angle.

To keep the mast from moving while the glue dries, take a lower shroud from each side, wrap it around a deadeye on the channels and hold it with an alligator clip. Make sure the masttop is parallel to the deck. If you do the job right all masts will be in line with each other athwartships because they'll be in line with the plumb line. Of course, every mast will have a different angle of rake, so you have to reset the line each time you set a mast.

The jig can be dismantled for storage.

STEPPING THE BOWSPRIT. After all the masts are in place, step the bowsprit. Most kits have predrilled holes in the stem of the hull through which to fit the bowsprit. You may have to file it slightly for a better fit. Your plans will indicate the distance from the baseline to the tip of the bowsprit; this will assure that the vertical angle (the *steeve*) of the bowsprit is correct. Apply a dab of glue to the base of the bowsprit and slide it in place, making sure that its steeve is correct. To check that its square athwartships, sight down the bowsprit from the front of the model at the masts. Apply a dab of ACC and let it set.

RIGGING IT ALL TO THE HULL

GETTING READY

Now that all the spars are fitted and rigged — and the masts and bowsprit stepped — we're ready to attach everything to the hull. How? Some lines will be belayed to pins, some will be bent to deadeyes, some will be seized (with our simple method, for now).

Rigging is an often delicate, sometimes annoying, and always rewarding task — if it's done right. Here are some tips that will save you a great deal of nail biting.

The key words when rigging are symmetry and balance. If you pull on one side, remember to counter it with an opposing pull. Before you start rigging on one side of the model, it's a good idea to tie a shroud temporarily to the deadeye on the other side. This will prevent the mast from bending while you are snugging up on the deadeye rigging and give you better looking, tighter shrouds.

Let's review the order in which everything will be rigged to the hull:

Step 1: Belay the yard lifts and halyards to their respective pins. Do not install yard braces at this time.

Step 2: Bend standing rigging in the following sequence: bowsprit bobstays, foremast stays to the bowsprit; all the mizzenmast gaffs and boom rigging; mainmast center stays to the foremast; and finally, the mizzenmast center stays to the mainmast.

Step 3: Rig all lower shrouds to their lanyards.

Step 4: Bend the backstays on each mast; the sequence doesn't matter.

Step 5: Install boats and davits, if called for.

Step 6: Fit and belay all yard braces.

AN EASY WAY. Much of the standing rigging is secured to lower deadeyes with lanyards. On real ships, the lanyard hauled taut the shrouds and kept them taut. That meant tying a stopper knot in the lanyard end and reeving it through alternate eyes, starting with the upper deadeye. After hauling taut, the end of the lanyard was run under itself to form a half hitch then wound around the stay or shroud. It was an effort that called more for muscle than finesse. Not so on a model.

Before we get started we should think about what we're doing. Just how do you attach a rope to a deadeye, in scale? Look at Figure 63 on page 102.

To make sure that the lanyards securing the shrouds are all the same length, we're going to make a "deadeye gauge" from a piece of pliable steel wire **(1)**. Bend the wire at right angles at each end — long enough to fit into and hold the upper and lower deadeyes that will be held by the lanyard. The straight part of the gauge should be about three times the diameter of the deadeyes.

For our purposes, attach the shrouds to the deadeyes beginning with the foremast, alternating port and starboard. Insert one end of the deadeye gauge in the middle hole of the upper deadeye and the other end into the middle hole of the lower deadeye **(2)**. Hold this in place with your left hand (if you're righthanded) and with your right, wrap the lower part of the shroud around the upper deadeye. Put tension on the shroud end while pulling upward. Move your left fingers up to catch and hold the two lines, and with your right hand use an alligator clip to hold them together.

Take a fine black rigging line and tie a double overhand knot around the shroud right above the upper deadeye. Apply a drop of glue to the knot and wrap the fine line around the shroud to seize it, ending with a clove hitch.

Here's how to reeve the lanyards through the deadeyes now held by the gauge. At the foremast, beginning on the port side, tie a double knot on the end of a fine black line and start threading

FIGURE 62. *Channels and deadeyes: where a lot of line meets a little space. Rigging through deadeyes is not as hard as it may appear.*

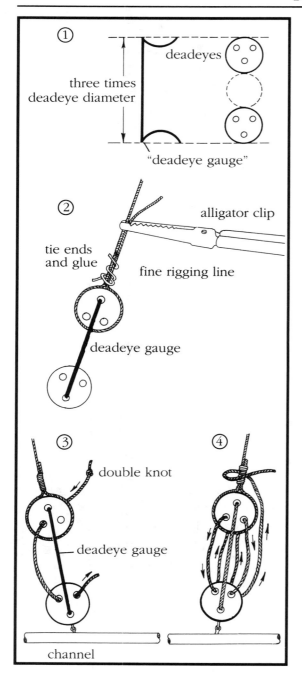

FIGURE 63. *Rigging shrouds the easy way.*

on the left hole of the upper deadeye and toward you. Next go through the left hole of the lower deadeye away from you **(3)**. At this point, remove the deadeye gauge and continue on through the rest of the holes **(4)**. Now pull down on the shroud with your left hand while pulling the lanyard up with your right hand to obtain the tension needed. Once this is accomplished and the deadeyes are set, tie the end of your lanyard around the shroud above the upper deadeye. Trim the excess line; apply a little glue and let dry.

Now that you've got that trick down (you may want to practice before trying it on your model), we're ready to actually start rigging everything. Here are some other things to keep in mind.

Never:
- cross rigging lines with each other
- run rigging lines on the forward side of the yards
- bend rigging lines around obstacles
- run rigging lines through ratlines
- make knots on rigging lines

STAYS

Place your hull (no need to remove it from its base) on a revolving stand. This will help immensely in turning the model around to reach for the belaying pins on the port or starboard side. Your best bet is a turntable from an old stereo system or a lazy Susan from the dinner table.

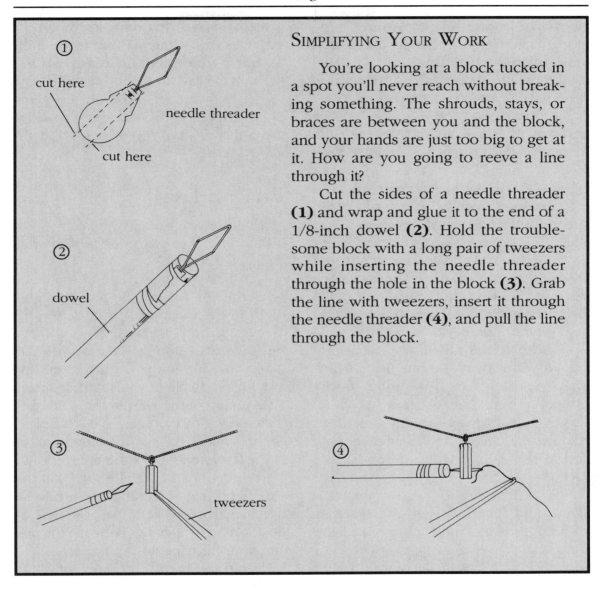

SIMPLIFYING YOUR WORK

You're looking at a block tucked in a spot you'll never reach without breaking something. The shrouds, stays, or braces are between you and the block, and your hands are just too big to get at it. How are you going to reeve a line through it?

Cut the sides of a needle threader (**1**) and wrap and glue it to the end of a 1/8-inch dowel (**2**). Hold the troublesome block with a long pair of tweezers while inserting the needle threader through the hole in the block (**3**). Grab the line with tweezers, insert it through the needle threader (**4**), and pull the line through the block.

Mount a plywood base on the turntable and you're set.

Begin with the innermost standing rigging on the bowsprit, such as the bobstays, jibstays, and martingale stays;

use the deadeye gauge and reeve the lanyards as we just discussed. Next, bend the foremast stays to the bowsprit and jibboom and serve them with an overhand knot in a shorter piece of line, just as we did earlier with the shrouds. Do not glue any knots or cut the excess line until everything is finished. This will enable you to readjust the stays' tension when all the rigging is finished.

After we bend and seize the foremast stays to the bowsprit, we'll secure the boom sheets and the gaff vangs to their belaying pins. This will set the proper aft tension on the mizzenmast so that it will not bend forward when we install the stays. Next rig the mainmast stays (on some ships, a mast could have as many as five stays) to the foremast, and the mizzenmast stays to the mainmast. Since no other rigging is in the way yet, it will be easier at this time to rig the lower stays to the blocks on deck.

On some ships the lower stays were rigged with *hearts* — sometimes heart-shaped, often round wooden blocks about the same size as deadeyes with a large multigrooved opening in their middles through which the lanyards were rove. Other ships used deadeyes or triple blocks.

Stays, like shrouds, were often set in pairs. And, like shrouds, the secret is making sure the stays are even at the deck. Here's a quick way to install your lower stays. Check the plans for the length of your stay and cut some black thread double that amount. Bend one end of the line around a block as dictated by the plans. Run the stay through the holes in the masttop, around the mast, and back down to the first block, where you'll bend the free end around

a second block. Put an alligator clip on the stays below the masttop to keep the assembly from slipping. Reeve lanyards through the two blocks to attach the stays to the bulwark according to the plans. Seize the two stays together above the alligator clip, serve them, and the stays are set.

BELAYING LINES

Most kits have a belaying pin plan. Study it beforehand to get an idea of the pattern you'll follow.

To belay a rigging line to a pin you wrap the line around the pin in a figure eight fashion, as we see in Figure 64. You'll need a belaying tool — you can buy one at a hobby shop or you can make one. If you opt for the latter, find a stiff wire, such as a wire clothes hanger. Heat the tip of the wire over a flame and flatten it with a hammer on a steel plate. With a small triangular file cut a groove at the flattened end of the wire to catch the rigging line **(1)**. Make sure that this part is not too wide and the groove is not too deep, otherwise you will be unable to insert the tool between the pins and wrap the line around them.

Hold the end of the line with your left hand (assuming you're righthanded) and with your right hand press the belaying tool to the line. Push the line under and around the pin **(2)**. Next turn the line across and around the pin above the rack, forming a figure eight **(3)**. Repeat two or three times **(4)**. Now twist the line

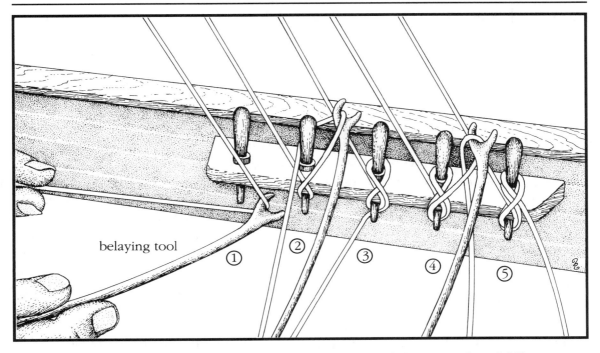

FIGURE 64. *Belaying lines to pins — make yourself a belaying tool and follow this sequence from left to right.*

with the two fingers of your left hand one turn to the left. This will cause the line to form a half hitch. Catch the line on the loop with the tool and set it on the pin **(5)**. Apply a dab of glue and let dry. Later you can cut the surplus line with a sharp knife and save it to make rope coils.

If you're installing sails on your model there will be more lines to be rigged on the pin racks set on the bulwarks. Check the plans and belay these lines now.

YARD LIFTS

On most ships the yard lifts were belayed to the pinrails around the base of the masts or to pin rings set around masts. To set the yards parallel to the deck and parallel to each other, use a ruler to measure the height of the ends of the lowest foremast yard from the caprail. Make sure each side is the same distance from the rail. Set the rest of the yards on the foremast using the same procedure, but measuring up from the yard below.

The mainmast and mizzenmast yards will be leveled, by sighting, to the foremast yards.

Halyards

Next come the halyards. Most halyards end with a purchase tied between two or more blocks and belayed to the bulwarks' pinrails or to rings on the deck.

Lower Shrouds

Now that the lifts, the halyards, the sails (if any), and their rigging are secured, we can work on the lower shrouds.

Rig the shrouds just as we discussed earlier in this section — using the deadeye gauge and the alligator clip. Use black line for the shrouds (they were tarred) and the lanyards. Lash sheerpoles above the deadeyes if your model calls for them.

Backstays

The backstays are tied down next. Follow the same method we used for the lower stays. Be careful not to pull so hard on the stays that you bend the mast sideways or backward.

Yard Braces and Sail Sheets

The yard braces and sail sheets are last. Belay the braces and sheets starting at the top of the foremast, moving down the mast. When the braces and sheets

on the foremast are belayed, move to the top of the mainmast and work down again. Then move on to the mizzenmast.

Rigging the braces between the main and mizzen is a bit challenging because the lines will cross. Take great pains to prevent them from bending and rubbing against each other. The easiest way is to alternate by rigging the braces of one yard to the main and one yard to the mizzen, checking that the lines do not rub or bend against each other.

While you're doing this you'll notice that it is very hard to reach the double blocks attached to the masts. You can use a long tweezer and a needle threader glued to the end of a dowel as we discussed.

When sails weren't attached, as in port, the yards usually were braced squarely. If you want your model to appear under sail, take great care when rigging the braces to set the angles of the yards. Yards were never braced at the same angle because the sails on one mast would move the apparent wind farther forward on the next mast aft. In fact, even sails on the same mast were not braced the same; the apparent wind moves aft as you go aloft, so that upper sails need not be braced as far around as the lowers.

If you decided not to use sails, set the highest yard on the foremast at the angle you prefer. (Sometimes a little bend to port or starboard makes the model look more interesting.) Set the rest of the yards on the foremast parallel or nearly

Photo 25. *A well-executed row of rope coils on the pin rails.*

so to the top yard by sighting from above. The angle of the yards on the main and mizzen will be more radical; the yards on individual masts, however, will be close to the same angle.

Do not belay the braces on the lower yards at this time if your model carries boats or davits. The davits and the boats must be installed before the lower yard braces.

The final touch to your rigging is to install rope coils on the belaying pins. After you make the rope coils (see page 67), install them using a long tweezer and a dab of glue.

PART IV
Finishing Her Up

"Young Officers sometimes feel a diffidence in soliciting information; either from a fear of exposing their ignorance, or from an idea that such a request may be treated with ridicule. A reference, like a work of this nature, which can be consulted with privacy, will obviate the difficulty: it was not a secondary consideration in the prosecution of it."

— A Young Sea Officer's Sheet Anchor, *1819*

That intricately rigged, finely crafted model now sitting in front of you knows you by now. It's watched your moods swing as you waded through the process. A while back you were a nervous novice, tentative, unsure about what to do next. Now you've got a nearly finished ship model at your fingertips; and you're feeling good, maybe even cocky.

That's fine, but don't get carried away; though you might feel like it, you're not finished yet. Stay with the cautious, careful streak we've been on

since we first laid the keel. A silly mistake now will throw some unwanted gloom into a festive moment.

Putting the finishing touches on your model is a lot like the proverbial icing on the cake. The cake might be delicious, but if the frosting is slopped on no one's going to notice.

The final touches will focus attention on your fine work, not detract from it. A smartly fitted anchor, an impeccable paint job, and nicely appointed boats and davits set off by a flying flag — these

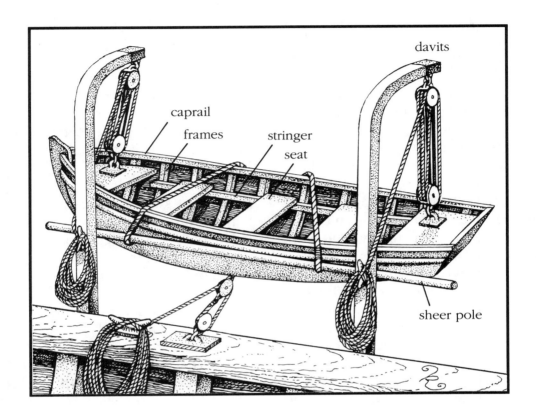

things can really add to your ship's looks. Take a deep breath and let's get going. We're almost there now.

BOATS, ANCHORS, PAINT, AND FLAGS

BOATS

Depending on its duties, a ship might have cause to use a number of boats —

service boats, fishing boats, and lifeboats. Some of the simpler boats were flat bottomed, some were planked smooth, and others were clinker-built or lapstraked (like a clapboard house).

Most kits provide small boats; some are precarved, some are stamped plywood plank-on-frame. Some kits just supply plans and instructions. Let's take a look at some of them.

Most of the precarved boats are pretty good — just the right size and shape — but they require additional work to make them look more authentic.

The first thing to do is to carve out the inside of the boat a little more. Use a small sanding drum on an electric drill at a reduced speed and then some gentle filing. Hand sand any rough spots, then stain or paint the inside.

Next install the frames. Make them from a thin wood strip; bend to match the curve of the hull and glue in place.

Install the floorboards and then the *stringers*. The stringers support the ends of the seats (or *thwarts*) and run parallel to the *gunwale* — the upper edge of the boat's side. Hold the stringers in place temporarily with small pins until the glue dries. The bow seat and the stern seat are made of thin (1 mm) plywood; cut the bow seat in a triangular shape and the stern seat in a "U" shape. Both can be planked for a better look. Bend the *caprail* — the top of the gunwale — along the boat's lines; drill two closely spaced holes in the caprail on each side of the boat midway between the seats and insert short pins in the holes to simulate *thole pins*, which accommodated oars in the days before oarlocks. Cut small wood triangles and erect them on the ends of the seats and against the hull to form reinforcing knees.

Now you can paint the outside of the boat.

Some kits will provide plank-on-frame boat kits. These can be very challenging — if not downright difficult — to build properly.

Why?

Some kits supply frames stamped on easily breakable 1 mm plywood. You also may find that some of the frames are so out of proportion that the finished hull looks like a cucumber. Another problem: you must remove the frames when the hull is completed, and this is no easy task. Then there are the frames that are too weak to support the planking. . . .

I am not saying that all plank-on-frame boat kits are impossible to build. Some can be constructed if you have a lot of patience and stamina. Following are some of the tricks that will help you accomplish it more readily:

- Make sure that the frames are centered on the keel properly before gluing.
- Cover the outside edges of the frames with masking tape so that the planks will not stick to them.
- Install a strip inside the frames as a temporary stringer to help keep the frames in place.
- Taper the planks just as you would on a ship model.
- Use double planking, making sure that the second layer of planks overlaps the seams on the first layer.
- After the planking is done remove the frames, sand the inside of the hull smooth, and install the ribs.
- If the boats look really bad, discard them and buy precarved ones.

Boats were stored on ships in different ways. Some were secured upside down on deckhouse roofs or on deck. The boats were set on two crosstimbers to avoid warping the keel and were lashed down with ropes to rings inserted on the timbers.

Some boats were set on cradles rightside up and lashed to the deck.

Some ships carried their service boats on *davits* — the arms used to hoist and hold the boat — fixed on the side or stern of the ship. A boat on davits will need blocks and tackles to be raised or lowered.

You can see a typical arrangement of a boat stowed on davits in the illustration on page 109. The davits can be installed either inboard or outboard. Some davits will swing inboard to stow the boat inside the ship. Davits were fitted with sheerpoles to prevent the boat from swinging in and out. In many cases. two lines ran from the pole around the boat, back to a block, and then to a purchase with the second block on the ship's caprail. There are variations on this arrangement; check your plans.

Some builders like to embellish the boats with in oars, buckets, and rudders — but it's not really authentic. On real ships this just wasn't done — they would all be washed overboard in the first rough seas.

DAVITS. Davits will vary with the ship and the era — some will be wooden, others metal. Watch out for the wooden ones because they sometimes are cut crossgrain and break at the slightest touch. If that's the case you can make your own, either by using your plank bender on a strip of wood the same size as the fragile kit davit or by cutting two halves on reverse grain and gluing them together.

ANCHORS

Anchors have undergone a lot of modification and improvement over the years — so it's important that you find the right one for your model. Again, a trip to the library will help. Some kits will supply woodstock that must be fitted around the upper portion of the anchor stock. After gluing the two halves together, you need metal loops, or something that looks like metal: Use thread or tape or even strips made from a sheet of shiny copper. Look at Figure 65.

Earlier, ships stowed their anchors outboard, lashing them to chainplates or to *bitts* — wooden posts — on the foredeck. Later the anchors were stowed inboard. The anchor was raised to the water surface by the *hawse cable* or *chain*; then it was raised to the *cathead* — a wood or metal beam at the bow — by, and this makes sense, the *cathead tackle*. Another tackle was then secured to one of the anchor's *flukes* and the anchor was hoisted over the bulwarks to its stowed position and lashed in place.

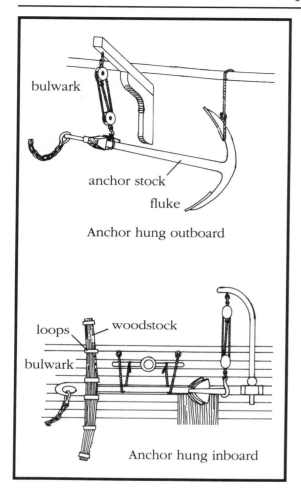

bulwark

anchor stock

fluke

Anchor hung outboard

loops

woodstock

bulwark

Anchor hung inboard

FIGURE 65. *Anchors — a finishing touch that deserves special care.*

FINISHING AND PAINTING

Depending on the period and style, you can leave your model in natural wood or you can paint it. Or you can do something in between — leaving it natural above the waterline and painted below.

I prefer as much as possible not to paint a model. The beauty of natural walnut contrasted with other woods such as limewood, boxwood, cherry, mahogany, or ebony is really something to rest your eyes on.

Avoid shiny finishes for period ship models: Don't use varnishes or oils, for they attract dust like a magnet.

To give your model the natural, raw look of old, use acrylic matte varnishes (decoupage), which you can find in art stores. Apply a first coat, let it dry, and then rub it with a very fine (0000) steel wool. Apply a second coat and again rub it with a very fine steel wool. If your model is a more modern craft you can use acrylic gloss medium and varnish.

These varnishes can also be used over acrylic base paint for a deeper tone and protection.

Preparing the surface of the wood will lead to better results. If you decide to paint, apply a coat of acrylic modeling paste with a stiff nylon brush until it is smooth. Be careful here — the paste dries hard, like fiberglass, and sanding off rough spots is a tough job. But painting over a surface treated with this paste is a blessing; it can be sanded eggshell smooth, and it prevents the paint from showing the wood grain.

Use water-soluble acrylic-base paints. There are no vapors, no streaks, and no messy brush cleaning. If you have to use petroleum-base paints, confine them to metal or very small areas. This kind of paint dries too quickly and is therefore almost impossible to brush smooth, and the vapors will not do much for your health. Here are some secrets for success in painting, especially with acrylic-base paints:

- Stir your paint well before using it. Pull out your stirring stick and watch how the paint drips off: You want a steady drip. Add a few drops of water if there's a slow drip, or no drip.
- Use only a sable-line brush; it won't leave any streaks on the paint.
- Apply the paint in one direction.
- Sand with fine wet-or-dry sandpaper between every coat.
- Apply a coat of matte varnish after the paint dries.
- Do not use steel wool on white painted surfaces.

Ships of the past were painted below the waterline with a mixture of tar, lead, or sulphur, which had an off-white color called tallow. You can reproduce this color by adding two or three drops of black and three to four drops of yellow to a container of two fluid ounces of white paint. Never use pure white paint.

It's a good practice to paint parts that will be installed on a nonpainted surface or on a surface of different color *beforehand*. If you can't, or if you forget, masking tape can help with straight lines and contrasting colors. (For example, painting the bulwarks.) But heed this: Don't apply masking tape to any painted surface unless it's had at least two

STICKY BOTTLE AND CAN CAPS

Try to unscrew a stubborn cap on a bottle of glue, varnish, or paint, and most likely you'll end up with a broken bottle, a bent cap, or a bleeding hand. Why not take a minute and a jar of petroleum jelly and avoid all the pain? Just apply some on the jar threads and screw the cap on again. Next time it will unscrew with a touch of your fingers. You'll also seal out the air and prevent the bottle's contents from hardening.

days to dry. For masking before painting, use Scotch fine-line tape, which you can buy in an autobody supply store; regular masking tape will leave a ragged edge. Do not remove the tape until the paint is dry. If you are going to paint around the inside frame of the gunports on the bulwarks, tape on the other side will prevent unwanted smudges around the edges.

FLAGS

Flags generally are supplied in your kit, often printed on silk and quite nicely made. But are they in scale?

Since flags are printed on silk or something similar, they fray when you cut around their edges. Apply a bit of diluted carpenter's glue where you wish to trim and let it dry before cutting.

Never install a flag by wrapping its edge around the tip of a mast or flag-staff. Wrap and glue the flag around a halyard fed through a block on top of the mast and tie the ends on the deck. Flags should be folded softly to look natural. You can wet the flag and wrap it around the shank of a hair-curling iron for a few seconds, and it will keep the natural look permanently.

ITALIAN-ENGLISH DICTIONARY

A

abete — spruce, fir
accesso — doorway, entrance
acessori — fittings
accetta — broad hatchet
acciaio — steel
acciarino — linchpin
accoppiatoio — coupling
accorciare — to shorten
accostare — to come alongside
accumulatore — storage battery
acero — maple
acido — acidity
acqua — water
adagio — easy
adattare — to fit
addestrare — to train
addietro — aft
adesivo — adhesive
adunare — to assemble
aeratore — aerator
aereo — aerial
aerodinamico — streamline
aeronave — hovercraft
aeroplano — aircraft
aeroporto — airport
affilare — to grind
affilato — sharp
affilatrice — grinder

affinare — to streamline
affogare — to drown
affondamento — sinking
affusto — mounting, gun-carriage
a galla — afloat
aggangiare — to hook
agghiaccio — steering gear
ago — needle
agucchia — sail needle
ala — wing
alabasso — downhaul
alafuori — outhaul (rope)
alare — to haul
alberamento — masting
alberatura — masts and yards
albero — mast
alesare — to bore, to ream
alga — seaweed
alighiero — gaff
alisei — tradewinds
allacciare — to lace, to seize
allagamento — to flood
allargare — to expand
allascare — to slacken
allentare — to loosen
allistamento — to fit out
allineamento — alignment
allineare — to line up
alloggi — berthing spaces
alluminio — aluminum

allungamento — lengthening
allungare — to lengthen
almezzo — amidship
alternatore — alternator
altezza — elevation, height
alto — tall
altoparlante — speaker
alzare — to lift, to raise
amaca — hammock
amantiglio — topping lift
amianto — asbestos
ammainare — to lower
ammiraglio — admiral
ancora — anchor
anello — ring
angolo — angle
annegare — to drown
annodare — to tie
antenna — lateen yard
antiaereo — anti-aircraft
antimonio — antimony
antiruggine — rust preserver
aperto — òpen
apertura — opening
apostolo — knighthead
apparato — outfit
apparecchio — mechanism, device
appendere — to hang
appiattire — to flatten
appoggio — support
apprezzamento — evaluation
approdare — to land
approntare — to get ready
aprire — to open
aquila — eagle
archetto — traveling iron
architettura — architecture
arganello — small capstan
argano — capstan
argento — silver
argilla — clay

arma — weapon
armamento — armament
armata — armada
arnesi — tools
arpone — harpoon
arredare — to fit out
arrembatori — boarders
arridatoio — turnbuckle
arrivare — to arrive at
arrontondare — to round out
arrotolare — to twist
arruginire — to rust
artiglieria — gunnery
ascia — ax
assemblaggio — assembling
assicurare — to insure
assottigliare — to fine off
asta — boom, staff, rod
attacco — attachment
attraversare — to go through
attrezzare — to rig
attrezzatura — rigging
attrezzo — rig
attrito — friction
automatico — automatic
avanti — ahead
avviso — warning
avvitare — to screw
avvolgere — to wind up
avvolgimento — winding
azione — action

B

bacchetta — rod
bacino — basin
baglietto — half beam, ledge
baglio — beam
bagnare — to wet
bagno — bath
balaustrata — poop rail, bulwarks

balaustri — fife rails
balconata — balcony
balena — whale
baleniera — whaling ship
balla — pack
balsa — balsa wood
banchina — dock, pier
banco — sand bank
banca — broadside
bandiera — flag
barca — boat
barcarizzo — gangway
barenare — to bore
barile — barrel
barra — bar, jack
barre — masthead
barrotto — hatch carling
basemento — base
bastardo — parrel rope
bastiere — sheer batten
bastimento — ship
bastinaggi — forecastle netting
bastone — boom
battaglia — battle
battagliola — bulwarks
battello — boat
battente — recess jamb
battere — to strike
batteria — electric battery
bava — burr
belvedere — mizzen topgallant sail
benzina — gasoline
bere — to drink
bersaglio — target
bertoccio — parrel truck
betulla — birch
bianco — white
bidone — barrel
biella — connecting rod
bigotta — dead eye
binario — rail track

binocolo — binoculars
bisellare — to bevel
bitta — bitt
bittalo — reefing bowsprit
bittone — bollard
bloccare — to block
boa — buoy
bobina — coil
bocca — mouth
boccaporto — hatch
boccola — bushing
bolina — bowline
bolzone — camber of beam
boma — sail boom
bombarda — bomb ketch
bordatura — beading
bosa — cringle
bosso — boxwood
botte barrel
bottiglia — bottle
bottone — button
bozza stopper
bozzello — block
braca — sling
braccio — arm
bracciolo — angle lug
bracotto — pendant
branca — bridle
branca — hammock
brasatura — to braze
brezza — breeze
brigantina — mizzen spanker
brignatino — brig
brilia — bobstay
bronzo — bronze
brunire — to polish
buco — hole
bugliolera — bucket rack
bugliolo — bucket
bullone — bolt
bussola — compass

buttafuoco — linstock
buttafuori — outrigger, bumpkin

C

cabina — cabin
cacciacavallo — fid, mast fid
cacciavite — screwdriver
calafatare — to caulk
calamita — magnet
calare — to lower
calore — heat
cambiare — to change
cambusa — storeroom
camera — room
camma — cam
campana — bell
campanile — bellfry
camuffamento — camouflage
canapa — hemp
candela — candle
candeliere — rail stanchion
canna — barrel
cannochiale — telescope
cannonata — gunshot
cannone — cannon
cannoniera — gunboat
canoa — canoe
canotto — boat
cantiere — shipyard
cantonale — bracket
capezziera — clew
capione — figurehead
capitano — captain
capobianco — untarred rope
capoc — kapok
capodibanda — rail, gunwale
cappa — hood
cappone — cathead
carabottino — grating
carbonara — mizzen staysail

carbone — coal
cardine — hinge
carena — ship's bottom
caricabbugna — clew, garnet
caricaboline — martinets
caricare — to haul
caricascotte — clew line
carpenteria — carpentry
carrello — carriage
carronata — carronade
carrozza campanionway
carrucola — puleggia — pulley
carta — map, paper
cartoccio — cartridge
casco — helmet
cassa — box
casseretto — poop, quarterdeck, afte-castle
cassero — bridge deck
castagna — pawl (capstan)
castagnola — cleat
castello — forecastle
catasta — pile
catena — chain
catramare — to tar
cavalla — topmast staysail
cavatoia — sheave, hole
cavetto — cable
cavicchio — wooden pin
caviglia — belayin pin
cavigliera — pin rail
cavo — cable, rope
cazzascotte — cleat, kevel
cedro — cedar
cella — cell
cementare — to cement
cenere — ash
cenerino — gray paint
centro — center
ceppi — leg irons
cerchiare — to hoop
cerchio — ring, hoop

cherchione — cannon hoop
cerniera — hinge
cerussa — white lead
cesoia — shear
cesta — crate
checcia — ketch
chiaro — clear
chiatta — barge
chiavarda — bolt
chiave — spanner, wrench
chiesuola — binnacle
chiglia — keel
chiodare — to rivet, to nail
chiodatura — riveting
chiodino — tack, small nail
chiodo — nail
chiudere — to shut
chiusura — closure
cianfrinare — to caulk
cielo — sky
ciliegio — cherry
cilindro — cylinder
cima — cable's end
cinghia — belt
cinta — binding strake
cipresso — cypress
circolo — circle
cisterna — tank
citta — town
ciurma — crew
classe — rate, class
clessidra — sand glass
clipper — clipper ship
cocca — cog, kink
coccinello — toggle
coda — tail
codice — code
cofano — casing, hood
coffa — mast top
cofferdam — bulkhead
colaggio — leakage

colla — glue, paste
collare — hoop
collegamento — connection, link
collegare — to connect
collicere — to bump
collo — ring
colamento — to fill up
colombiere — mast head
colonna — pillar, column
colpi — hammer strikes
colpire — to hit
coltellaccino — topgallant, studding sail
coltellaccio — studding sail
coltello — knife
colubrina — culverin, galley gun
combaciare — to match
combustione — combustion
comento — seam
cominciare — to begin
compartimento — compartment
compasso — compass
complesso — assembly
componente — component
conca — basin
concatenamento — linkage
conchiglia — shell
conciare — to tan
condensare — to condense
condotta — piping
condotto — flue, pipe
congegno — gear
cona — cone
contagocce — dropper
contatto — contact
contenitore — container
contenuto — content
contorno — outline
controaereo — anti-aircraft
contramante — preventer tie
contramantiglio — preventer lift
controanello — clamang ring

controbelvedere — mizzen royal
controbraccio — preventer brace
controchiglia — upper keel
controcoperta — spar deck
controcorsia — fore and aft carling
controdado — lock nut
controdragante — helm transom
contro fasciare — to double plank
contro fiocco — flying jib
controlanda — preventer chain plate
contromarciapiede — yard arm horse
contromezzana — mizzen topsail
contromezzana bassa — mizzen lower topsail
contromezzana volante — mizzen upper
    topsail
contropiastra — guard plate
contropicco — ensign gaff
controportello — cargo door
controranda — gaff
controranda di mezzana — mizzen gaff topsail
controranda di trinchetto — fore gaff topsail
controruota — inner stem
contro sartia — preventer shroud
controstaglio — preventer backstay
controvelaccino — fore royal
controvelaccio — main royal
convertire — to convert
convesso — cambered
copale — varnish
coperchio — cover, lid
coperta — main deck
copertino — steel deck plate
copertura — coverage
coppa — cup
coppia — couple
coppiglia — cotter pin
corazza — armor
corba — frame
corda — rope, line
cordame — cordage
corno — horn

corona — ring
coronamento — taff rail
corpo — body
corredare — to equip
correggia — belt
corridoio — alleyway
corridore — lanyard
corrodere — to corrode
corroso — pitted
corsaro — raider
corsia — header
corso — strake
corsono — sliding block
cortina — screen
costa — frame, rib
costa — seacoast
costola — frame
costruire — to build
costruzione — construction
cotone — canvas, cotton
convertetta — orlop deck
cravatta — bridle
cremagliera — rack
cricca — crack
croce — cross
crocette — crosstrees
crociame — spars
crogiuolo — melting pot
cromatura — chromium plating
cuscino — pillow

D

dado — nut
damigiana — carboy
danneggiamento — damage
dara — booms, spars
dardo — harpoon
dare — to give

darsena — closed dock
data — date
davanti — ahead
decrescente — decreasing
deflettore — baffle
deformazione — deformation
delfiniera — dolphin striker
demolire — to break up
densita — density
dentato — toothed
dente — tooth, bill
dente di fissagio — snug
dente c'incastro — cog
dente di ruota — sprocket
depurare — to filter
deriva — drift
destri — round house
detonante — priming mixture
devastare — to rake
deviazione — deflection
diaframma — baffle plate
diagonale — diagonal
diagramma — graph
diametro — diameter
dicco — dock
dicontra — skysail
dicontra di contromaestra — middle skysail
dicontra di contromezzana — jigger skysail
dicontra di maestra — main skysail
dicontra di mezzana — mizzen skysail
dicontra di trinchetto — fore skysail
dicontra di volante — flying skysail
diesel barca — diesel launch
difensa — rope guard
difetto — faulty defect
differenza — difference
diferrimento — postponement
diga — duke
dilatare — to expand
dilettanto — amateur
diluente — thinner

diluire — to thin
dimensione — dimension, size
diminuire — to shorten
di punta — head and head
diramazione — branch
direzione — direction, bearing
dirigere — to steer
disalberare — to dismast
disarmato — off-center
disbittare — to unbitt
discesa — fall
disco — disk
discolcato — gunwale, drift-rack
disegnare — to draw
disegno — drawing
dislocamento — displacement
discolare — to displace
disossidante — deoxidizer
dispensa — storeroom
dispersione — scattering
disposizione — arrangement
dissaldare — to solder
disseccare — to dry out
distaccare — to detach
distanza — distance
distendere — to stretch
distintivo — pennant
distorzione — distortion
divisione — division
documenti — papers
doche — barrel staves
doppia prora — double ender
doppiare — to double
doppir — twofold
doppio fondo — double bottom
dorata — golden
dormiente — beam
dormiente dei bagli — sleeper beam
dormiente dei castelli — string beam
dormiente dicoperta — deck beam
dormiente di stiva — hold beam

dormiente del ponte inferior — lower deck beam

dorsale — ridge

dorso — back

draglia — rope stay

dritta — starboard

dritto — post

drizza — halyard

droma — spars

duomo — dome

dura — stiff

durezza — hardness

E

ebano — ebony

eccentricita — eccentricity

efficienza — efficiency

elasticita — elasticity

elevare — to raise

elevatore — lift

elevazione — height

elica — propeller

energia — power

errore — error

esaminare — to survey

escludere — to cut out

espandere — to expand

esponente — index

essere — to be

essiccante — drier

est — east

estrarre — to draw off

estremita — end

F

fabbrica — mill, factory

fabro — blacksmith

faccia — face, surface

falchetta — gunwale

falconetto — falconet

falla — breach

falso — dummy

fasciare — to plank

fasciatura — wrapping, serving

fatica — labor

fattore — factor

feltro — felt

femminella — gudgeon brace

fendere — to split

fenditura — crack

feritoia — loop hole

fermare — to stop

ferzo — sailcloth

fessura — crack

fiaccola — torch

fiamma — flame, pennant

fiancata — broadside

fianco — side

fighiera — jackstay

filaccia — rope yarn

filare — rail

filetto — thread

filo — twine, thread

filtro — filter

fine — end

finestra — window

finire — to finish

finezza — fineness

fiocco — jib

fiocina — hand harpoon

fischio — whistle

fissaggio — fastening

fiume — river

flangia — flange

flessibilita — flexibility

flotta — fleet

focolare — furnace, fire-box

focone — vent

fodera — sheathing

foderare — to sheath

fodero — bucket
fondazione — foundation
fondita — casting
fontana — fountain
fonte — hatchway, cockpit
forare — to bore
foratura — drilling
forbici — belaying cleat, kevel
forcella — yoke
forchetta — fork
forgia — forge
formare — to form
formatura — moulding
forme — rib bands
fornire — to supply
forno — furnace
foro — hole
fortezza — belly band
forza — force
forzare — to strain
fragile — brittle
frascone — garnet
frassino — ashwood
frattura — fracture
freccia — gaff topsail
fregio — carved work
frenello — tiller rope-T. chain
fresare — to mill
frisata — gunwale
fucina — forge
fuga — escape
fulcro — fulcrum
fumaiolo — funnel
fumiera — smoke-box
fumo — smoke
fune — rope
funzionamento — operation
funzionare — to work
fuochi — fires
fuoribordo — outboard boat
fuoriscalmo — outrigger

fusione — casting
fusto — drum

G

gabbia — topsail
gabbia di contromezzana — jigger topsail
gabbia di contromaestra — middle topsail
gabbia di mezzana — mizzen topsail
gabbia di trinchetto — fore topsail
gabbia di maestra — main upper topsail
gaffa — gaff, pole hook
gaggia — top castle
galea — galley
galeone — galeon
gallegiabile — buoyant
galleggiamento — floatation
galleggiante — float
galleggiare — to float
galleria — alley, tunnel
galletto — wing nut
galloccia — cleat, cavil
gallone — gallon
galtella — bibb
gamba — transom
gambo — shank
ganascia — brake shoe
gancetto — hook
gancio — hook
garanzia — warranty
garbo — template
gaschetta — reefing
gassa — eyesplice
gavitello — buoy, float
gelare — to freeze
gelo — frost
gemello — twin
generare — to generate
generatore — generator
gente — crew, people
gerco — gasket

gettare — to throw

gettata — jetty

getto — casting

gherlino — hawser, towline

gherone — girt band

ghia — cargo line

ghiaccio — ice

ghiaia — gravel

ghindaggio — hoisting

ghindare — to hoist

ghindaressa — mast rope

ghindata — hoist

ghindazzo — heel tackle

ghirlanda — deck hook

ghisa — cast iron

giacca — jacket

giardinetti — quarter gallery

giglio — lily flower

ginocchio — turn of the bilge

gioco — clearance

giogo — yoke

giorno — day

giarabecchino — brace

girante — rotor

girare — to turn

giratoio — swivel hook

giro — turn

girobussola — gyro compass

girone — handle

giropilota — automatic steerer

girostato — gyrostat

girotta — rudder yoke

giunta — butt, joint

giunto — coupling

giuntura — butt seam

giunzione — seam

glifo — link block

globo — globe

gola — groove

goletta — schooner

golfare — eye bolt

golfo — bay

gomena — hawser-cable

gomenetta — cable-laid rope

gomito — elbow

gomma — rubber

gonfiamento — swelling

gonfiare — to swell

gottazza — scoop

gotto — pump box

governare — to steer

gradino — step

grado — rank

graffa — claw, brace

grafico — diagram

grafite — black lead

grampia — dog iron

grandezza — size

grappa — clip

grappino — grappling iron

grasso — grease

graticola — fire grate

gratile — boltrope

grattare — to scrape

grava — strand

grondaia — chute, spout

grosso — big

grua — crane

gruetta — bumpkin

gruppo — cluster, bunch

guancia — bow

guanciale — bolster

guanto — glove

guardacorpo — lifeline

guardamano — guard-rope

guarnimenti — gear

guarnitura — fitting

fuarnizione — gasket

guasto — breakdown

guglia — pinnacle

guide — guide

guscio — shell

I

idrometro — water gauge
illuminazione — lighting
imballaggio — packing
imbando — slack
imbarcadero — landing place
imbarcazione — ship's boat, craft
imbiancare — to whiten
imbigottare — to turn in a deadeye
imbittare — to bitt
imboccalore — to fit with a sleeve
imbuto — funnel
immagine — image, picture
immergere — to dip, to immerge
impagliettare — to mat
impalcato — decking
impanatura — thread
impavesare — to dress ship
impavesata — bulwark
impavesate — hammock netting
impeciare — to pitch
impermeabile — waterproof
imperniare — to bolt
impianti — installations
impiombare — to splice
impiombatura — splice
impugnatura — handle
incamiciatura — lining
incandescente — red hot
incappellaggio — crance-iron
incastrare — to mortise
incastro — mortise
incatramare — to tar
incavigliare — to fasten
incavo — notch
incendiare — to set afire
incerata — tarpaulin
inchiocare — to nail
incinta — ship's wale

incisore — engraver
inclinare — to lean
inclinazione — trim of masts
incocciare — to hook
incollare — to glue
incrinare — to crack
incroce — squared
incrociare — to cross
incrocinatore — cruiser
incrostazione — scaling
incudine — anvil
incuneare — to wedge
incurvare — to bend
indicatore — recorder
indice — index
indietro — astern
inferire — to lace
infilare — to feed through
infossature — runnels
infrazione — breach
inghinare — to lash
ingobbare — to bulge
ingobrante — bulky
ingombro — hamper
ingrannaggio — gear
ingrassaggio — greasing
ingrisellare — to rattle
ingrossare — to grow
innesto — clutch
inondare — to flood
inossidabile — inoxidable
insellamento — sagging
insellatura — sheer
inserire — to insert
installare — to install
insufflare — to inflate
intaccare — to groove
intagli — carvings
intagliare — to carve
intasare — to block, to jam
intelaiatura — framework

intercapedine — interspace
interni — interiors
interponte — between decks
interrompere — to disconnect
interruzione — breaking
intestare — to butt a joint
intrecciare — to twist
introdurre — to insert
intugliare — to knot two ropes
invasare — to put on the cradle
invelare — to clothe a vessel, spread sail
inventario — inventory
invergatura — luff-rope
invertire — to reverse
invoglia — parcelling
involucro — casing
irrigidimento — to straighten
irrobustire — to strengthen
isola — island
isolante — insulation
istruzioni — instruction

L

laboratorio — workshop
lacca — lacquer
lacerare — to rip
lama — blade
lamiera — plate
laminare — to laminate
laminazione — cold rolling
lampada — lamp
lampadina — bulb
lascare — to slack
lasciare — to let
lastrone — sheet
lato — side
latrina — latrine
lattina — a can, container
lavaggio — washing
lavare — to wash

lavorare — to work
lavoro — work, job
leccio — evergreen oak
lega — alloy
legamento — binding
legare — to tie
legname — wood, timber
legno — wood
legnolo — rope strand
lente — glass, lens
lenza — fishing line
lesina — sewing awl
lesione — leak
leso — tap bolt
lettera — letter
letto — bed
lettura — reading
leva — lever
levante — orient, east
levigare — to smooth
lezzino — marline, marling
libbra — pound
liberare — to free
libero — open, clear
libo — lighter
libretto — little book
lignite — brown coal
lima — file
limaccioso — slimy
limare — to file
limatura — file dust
limite — limit
lingotto — ingot
linguella — baffle plate
lino — flax
liquefare — to melt
liquido — liquid, fluid
lishiare — to smooth
lista — list
listello — band, fillet
listone — planksheer

litro — liter
livella — level
livello — level gauge
locale — space, room
localizzare — to spot
logoramento — wear
lombolo — bilge
longarina — ribband
longiterone — spring beam
longitudinale — longitudinal
lontano — far away
losca — rudeer well
lotto — parcel
luce — light
lucidare — to polish
lume — lantern
luna — moon
lunetta — bell chuck
lunghezza — length
luogo — place
lupa — strainer plate

M

macchina — engine
macchinario — machinery
macchinista — engineer
madiata — log-raft
madiere — floor plate
madrevite — screw die
magazzino — warehouse
maglia — chain link
maglietto — maul, hammer
magnete — magnet
malleabile — malleable
mancare — to miss
mancina — crane
mandare — to send
mandata — discharge
mandola — bull's eye
mandrinare — to expand

mandrino — expander
maneggiare — to handle
manichetta — spout, hose
manico — handle
manicotto — sleeve
maniglia — shackle
manilla — manila (rope)
mano — hand
manometro — pressure gauge
manopola — knob
manovella — crank
manovra — operation, maneuver
mantelletto — port lid
mantello — shell
mantice — bellows
manuale — handbook
manubrio — handle
manutenzione — maintenance
mappa — chart, map
mappamondo — globe
marcare — to mark
marchio — branding iron
marcia — march
marciapede — footrope
mare — sea
marea — tide
margherita — sheep-shank
margine — edge
marinaio — seaman
martellare — to hammer
martello — hammer
martinetto — jack
masca — bow
mascella — saw
maschera — mask
maschetta — mast cheek
maschiare — to tap
maschio — nut
mascolo — chambered block
mascone — bow
massa — mass, weight

mastice — cement
mastra — coaming
matafione — roband
materia — subject
mattone — brick
mazza — sledge hammer
mazzetta — headrope
massuolo — mallet
meccanismo — gear
megafono — speaking tube
mensola — bracket
merlino — marlin
metallo — metal
metrico — metric
metro — measuring tape
mettere — to put
mezzagalera — half galley
mezzana — crossjack
mezzanella — mizzen, jigger
mezzanino — hatch beam
mezzavela — raffee (half gaff sail)
mezzi — means
mezzoponte — raised deck
mezzotondo — half round bar
miglio — mile
mimetizzare — to camoflage
mina — mine
minerale — ore
minio — red-lead
minuto — minute
mira — aim
mirare — to aim
miscela — mixture
misura — measure
mitragliera — machine gun
modanatura — moulding
madano — spool
modellismo — modelling
modello — model
mogano — mahogany
mola — grinding wheel

molare — to grind
molla — spring
montacarichi — elevator
montaggio — assembling
montare — to assemble
mordace — vile clamp
morsa — vice
mortaretto — pump box
mortasa — mortise
mortisa — fid-hole
moto — motion
motobarca — motorboat
motolancia — motorlaunch
motonave — motorship
motopeschereccio — motor fishing vessel
motopompa — motor pump
motore — engine
motoscafo — motorboat
motrice — engine
movimento — motion
mozzo — ring bolt
mulinello — windlass
munizioni — ammunition
mura — tack
murare — to haul
mure — tacks
muro — wall
mutamento — shifting

N

naso — nose
nastro — tape
navale — naval
nave — ship
navigare — to sail
nazione — nation
nebbia — fog
nemico — enemy
nervatura — bead
netto — clean

neve — snow
nicchia — recess
noce — walnut
nodo — knot
nome — name
nord — north
nota — note
notte — night
nube — cloud
nucleare — nuclear
numero — number
nuotare — to swim

O

obiettivo — target
oblo — porthole
occhiello — eyelet
occhio — eye
occidente — west
occultare — to conceal
oceano — ocean
officina — workshop
oggetto — subject matter
olio — oil
olivo — olive
onda — wave
ondulato — rippled
opera — works
operaio — worker
operatore — operator
ora — hour, time
orbita — orbit
ordinate — frame, rib
ordine — order
orecchia — cleat
orecchione — trunnion
organi — components
oriente — east
orizzonte — horizon
orlo — edge, trim

ormeggi — moorings
ornamento — moulding
orologio — clock
orza — luff
oscurare — to darken
ospedale — hospital
osservare — to sight
osservatore — observer
ossidabile — oxidable
ossidare — to oxidize
ossigeno — oxygen
ostacolo — hamper
osteriggio — skylight
ostino — vang, guy
ostruzione — barrier
ottica — optics
ottone — brass
otturare — to choke up
ovest — west

P

pacco — parcel
padiglione — rigging
pagaia — paddle
paglietto — mat
pagliolato — floorboards
paiuolo — guns platform
pala — shovel, blade
palamite — troll line
palanca — gangway
palancare — to bowse
palanchino — crow bar
palco di comando — bridge
palella — paddle
palissandro — rosewood
palla — bullet, cannon ball
palliera — shot-rack
pallone — balloon
palo — pole
palombaro — diver

paluce — marsh
pancia — bilge, belly
pane — bread
panfilio — yacht
paniere — basket
pannello — panel-board
panno — hatch-cover
pappafico — fore-topgallant-sail
parabordo — bumper
paraelica — propeller guard
paraffina — wax
parafulmine — lightning rod
paraghiacchio — ice fender
parallele — parallel rules
paramarre — anchor chock
paramezzale — keelson
paranchino — jigger-tackle
paranco — tackle
perdere — to lose
perdita — loss
perforare — to drill
pericolo — danger
periferico — peripheral
perimetro — perimeter, girth
periodo — period, cycle
periscopio — periscope
perla — pearl
perno — bolt, pin
pernone — gudgeon
pernotto — rivet
peppendicolare — perpendicular
pesare — to weigh
pesca — fishing
pescaggio — draft
pescatore — fishing tackle
peschereccio — fishing boat
peso — weight
petroliera — oil tanker
pezzo — gun, cannon
pezzo — part, component
pialla — plane

piallare — to plane
pianeta — planet
piano — chart, plan
piano — flush
piano — slowly
pianta — layout
piastra — plate
piastrina — shimstock
piattaforma — platform
piatto — plate
piazzale — area
picchettaggio — scaling
picco — gaff, peak
picozza — broad axe
piede — foot, heel
piedestallo — pedestal
piedistallo — pillow-block
piegare — to fold, to furl
piegato — indented
piegatura — bending
piena — full
pietra — stone
pigna — pump strainer
pignone — pinion
pila — battery
pilastro — pillar
pinnacolo — pinnacle
pino — pine
pinta — pint
pinza — crow-bar
pinze — pliers
pioggia — rain
piolo — — pin, rung
piombo — lead
pioppo — poplar
piovere — to rain
pipa — pipe
pirata — pirate
pirobarca — steam launch
piroscafo — steamer
piscina — swimming pool

pispagno — pitch-pine
pista — ball race, trck
pistola — pistol
pistone — piston
pittura — paint
pitturale — to paint
piuolo — rung (ladder)
placca — plate
plancia — bridge
polaccone — spinnaker
polena — figurehead
pollice — inch
polo — pole
polvere — powder, dust
polveriera — powder-magazine
pompa — pump
pompare — to pump
ponente — west
ponte — deck, bridge
pontile — pier
pontone — barge
pontuale — sleeper
poppa — stern
poppavia — aft, astern
porta — door, gate
portacaviglie — spider band
portapalle — shot-rack
portata — load capacity
portellino — light-port
portello — port, opening
porto — harbor
posizione — position
posta — mail
posto — station
potenza — horsepower
prendere — to take
preparato — compound
pressare — to press
pressatrecce — gland, stuffing box
pressione — pressure
prezzo — price

procedere — to proceed
procedimento — process
prodotti — products
produzione — output
profilato — section-bar
profondita — depth
profondo — deep
progettare — to plan
progetti — plans
progredire — to make headway
proietto — shell
proiezione — projection
prolunga — extension
prolungare — to extend
pronto — ready
propulsione — propulsion
propulsore — propeller
prora — bow, stem
proravia — forward
proseguire — to proceed
proteggere — to protect
prova — test, trial
provare — to test
prove — tests, trials
provviste — stores, supply
prua — bow
puleggia — pulley
pulizia — cleaning
pulsante — pushbutton
punizione — punishment
punta — point, bit
puntale — pillar
puntamento — aiming
puntare — to point, to aim
punteggiare — to point
puntellamento — strutting
puntellare — to prop
puntelli — tree timbers
puntello — strut
punteruolo — awl, stabber
punto — point

punzonare — to punch
punzone — hand punch

Q

quaderno — book
quadraggio — hatch square
quadrante — quadrant
quadrato — square
quadrello — lining cloth
quadro — panel board
qualita — qualities
quarantina — quarantine
quartabuono — bevel
quarto — quarter
quattro — four
quercia — oak
quinto — frame, timber
quota — depth
quotatura — dimensioning

R

rabazza — heel — (mast)
raccolta — gangway
racconciare — to mend
raccontare — to tell
raccorciare — to shorten
raccordare — to connect, to joint
raccord — pipe fitting
raddobbare — to refit
raddoppiamento — doubling, lining
raddoppiare — to double
radunare — to collect, assemble
raffica — wind gust
raffilatoio — spoke-shave
raffio — crow-bar
rafforzare — to strengthen
raffreddamento — cooling
raggio — arm, radius
ragna — crowfoot

ralinga — bolt-rope
ralla — half bearing
rallentamento — deceleration
rallentare — to decelerate
ramaio — coopersmith
ramato — coppered
rame — copper
ramificazione — branch
ramo — branch
rampa — ramp
rampino — grapnel
rampone — harpoon
randa — mainsail
rapportatore — protractor
rapporto — ratio
raschiatolo — scraper
raschietta — scaler
raso — flush
raspa — rasp
raspare — to rasp
rastrellamento — raking
rastrellare — to drag
rastrelliera — rack
rastrello — drag, rake
rastremare — to taper
rata — rate
rattoppare — to patch
rattoppo — patch
razione — allowance
razzo — rocket
reale — royal galley
reattore — reactor, jet
reazione — reaction
recipiente — can, container
redan — step
redancia — thimble
redazza — mop, deck mop
redazzare — to swab
refrattario — refactory
refrigerante — coolant
refrigeratore — cooler

regata — race, regatta
reggimano — hand-rail
reggiscosse — buffer, bumper
reggispinta — shock absorber
regione — area, zone
registratore — recorder
registro — book, log
registro — damper
regola — rule, method
regolatore — governor control
regolo — straight edge rule
relitti — wreckage
relitto — wreck
remi — oars
rena — sand
residuo — residue
resina — resin
resistenza — drag
restare — to lay, to rest
rete — netting, network
reticella — gauze (wire)
reticolato — grid
retrocedere — to back up
rettificare — to correct
revisione — overhaul
rialberare — to remast
ribattino — rivet
ribuzzo — drive bolt
ricalafatare — to recalk
ricerca — search
ricerche — researches
ricevere — to receive
ricoprimento — overlapping
ricostruire — to rebuild
ricovero — shelter
ricuocere — to anneal
ricuperare — to salvage
ricupero — salvage
rida — lanyard
riduttore — reducer
riduzione — reduction

riempimento — filling
riflettore — reflector
riga — rule, straight edge
riggia — futtock, shroud
righino — rubbing, strake
rigidezza — stiffness
rimontaggio — to reassemble
rimorchio — tow
rinculare — to recoil
rinforzo — stiffener
ringhiera — rail, handril
riparare — to fix
ripetere — to repeat
riposo — rest
riposteria — pantry
ripostiglio — locker
riprendere — to recover
ripristinare — to restore
riquadratura — square-butting
riscaldamento — heating
rischi — risks, perils
rispetti — spare-stores
ritagli — crop-ends
ritardare — to lag, to delay
ritegno — stop
ritenuta — breeching, check-ropes
ritiro — shrinkage
ritornare — to come back
ritorno — hauling end
riva — shore
rivelare — to detect, to uncover
riverniciare — to repaint
rivestimento — furring, sheathing
rivestire — to coat, to sheath
rivetto — rivet
rivolta — mutiny
rizza — lashing
rizzare — to lash, to secure
rizzatura — frapping, lashing
robustezza — strength
rocchetto — coil, reel

roccioso — rocky
rollare — to roll, to reel
rompighiaccio — icebreaker
rondella — washer
rosa — rose
rosetta — washer
rosso — red
rotaia — rail
rotante — rotary
rotazione — turn
rotella — winch drum
rotolare — to roll
rotore — rotor
rotta — course
rottame — wreckage
rotto — broken
rovere — quercia
rovesciare — to tip
rovesciato — upside down
rubare — to steal
rubinetto — cock, valve
ruggine — rust
rugiada — dew
rugosita — roughness
rullo — roller
rumenta — garbage
ruota — wheel

S

sabbia — sand
sabbiatura — sandblasting
sacca — pocket
sacchetto — small bag
sacco — bag
sagola — lanyard
sagoletta — string
sagomare — to shape
sagomatura — shaping
sala — room
salda — dura, strong

saldare — to solder
saldatoio — soldering iron
saldatrice — welder
saldatura — weld
sale — salt
saletta — officers' mess
salire — to rise
salpare — to weigh anchor
salsola — kelp
saltare — to jump
salto — rise, lift
salutare — to salute
salva — volley, salute
salvare — to rescue
sambuco — elder
sano — sound
santabarbara — powder magazine
saracco — handsaw
saracinesca — sluice-valve
sartia — shroud
sassola — scoop
sballare — to unpack
sbandamento — list, heeling
sbandare — to list
sbarcare — to land
sbarra — bus-bar
sbarzamento — obstruction
sbarrare — to block
sbieco — skew
sbirro — strap, strop
sbracare — to unsling
sbullonare — to unbolt
scafandro — diving gear
scafo — hull, craft
scaglia — scale
scala — ladder, gangway
scaldare — to warm, to heat
scalinata — staircase
scalino — step
scalmi — timbers
scalmiera — rowlock

scalmo — oar-pin
scalmotto — stanchion
scalo — dock, berth
scalpellare — to chip, to chisel
scalpello — chisel
scalzare — to undermine
scambio — exchange
scanalare — to groove, to slot
scanalatura — furrow, rabbet
scandagli — soundings
scannellare — to channel
scannellatura — rabbet
scanno — bar
scantonare — to chamfer
scappavia — galley
scappellare — to unbitt, to unrig
scarica — discharge
scaricabombe — depth-charge-rail
scaricare — to unload
scarico — exhaust, discharge
scarpa — fluke chock
scassa — mast step, step
scatola — box, case
scatto — release
scendere — to come down
scheggia — splinter
scheggiare — to chip, to splinter
scheletro — skeleton
schema — diagram
schermare — to shield
schermo — baffle
schienale — backrail
schiodare — to unrivet
schiuma — foam
scia — wake
sciabola — sword
scialuppa — sailboat
sciarpa — sash
scienze — sciences
scintilla — spark
scintillare — to sparkle

sciogliere — to untie
sciopero — strike
scivolare — to slip
scivoro — skidway, skate
scocciare — to unhook
scodella — bowl, saucer
scodellino — cup
scogli — rocks
scogliera — reef
scolo — drain
scoltura — carved work
scopa — broom
scopamare — lower-studding-sail
scoperta — discovery
scoppiare — to blow up, to burst
scoria — scale
scorrere — to flow, to slide
scotta — sheet (sail brace)
scovolo — swab, brush, tube brush
screpolatura — crack, flaw
scriccare — to chip
scucire — to unseam
scudare — to shield
scudo — shield
scuola — school
scure — ax, broadax
secca — shoal
seccare — to dry up
secchio — pail, bucket
sede — seat
sedia — chair
sedile — seat
sedimento — deposit, scale
sega — saw
segaccio — ripsaw
segare — to saw
segetto — handsaw
segnale — signal
segnare — to mark
segno — mark
seguire — to follow

sella — seating, bearer, base

semaforo — semaphore

semicerchio — semi-circle

semitondo — half-round bar

senso — direction

sentina — bilge

sentinella — sentry

serbatoio — tank, reservoir

serie — set, row

serpentino — pipe coil

serrabozze — cathead stopper

serracavi — cable clamp

serrafilo — wire clamp

serragiunto — screw-clamp

serranda — damper

serrapennone — leech-line

serrare — to furl, to close

serratura — lock

serretta — batten

serrette — bottom-boards

serrettoni — thick strakes

sesta — template

sestante — sextant

sesto — model, template

settore — quadrant

sezione — section, department

sfera — globe, ball

sfiatatoi — venting system

sfilacce — old-rope yarns

sfilacciare — to untwist

sfoderare — to unsheathe

sfogo — vent

sfondatoio — auger

sforzo — stress, strain

sfregare — to chafe, to rub

sfuggire — to escape

sgangiare — to release

sgombrare — to clear

sgranare — to uncouple

sgrossatura — roughing

sicurezza — safety

sicuro — reliable, safe

sifone — siphon

sigillare — to seal

sigillo — seal

silenzio — silence

silice — silica

silo — storage bin

siluro — torpedo

simbolo — symbol

simmetria — symmetry

simmetrico — symmetrical

sinistra — portside

sinistro — accident

sintonizzare — to tune up

sirena — siren, mermaid

siringa — syringe

sistema — system

siviera — ladle

slacciare — to unlace

slancio — overhang

slegare — to unlash

slitta — slide

slittamento — shifting

smaltare — to enamel

smanigliare — to unshackle

smantellamento — dismantling

smantellare — to dismantle

smerigliare — to grind

smeriglio — emery paper

smontare — dismantle

smorzatore — damper

smussare — to bevel

snodare — to unknot

snodo — joint

soccorso — assistance

societa — company, firm

soda — soda

sodio — sodium

soffiante — blower

soffiare — to blow

soffietto — bellows

soffittatura — ceiling, overhead
soffocamento — smothering
soffacare — to smother
soglia — sole, sill, sheerstrake
solco — grove
soldo — money
sole — sun
solfato — sulphate
sollevamento — lifting
sollevare — to hoist, to lift
solstizio — solstice
soluzione — solution
solvente — solvent
sommergere — to submerge
sommergibile — submarine
sommergibile — submersible
sonar — sonar
sonda — gauge, probe
sondaggio — sounding
sopracqueo — above-water
soprastruttura — superstructure
sordina — camper
sorgere — to rise
sorpresa — surprise
sorveglianza — survey
sospensore — sling
sospeso — overhung
sostegno — support, bearer
sostenere — to support
sostituire — to replace
sostituzione — replacement
sottacqua — underwater
sottigliezza — thinness
sottochiglia — false keel
sottocoperta — below deck
sottogavone — peak tank
spaccare — to split
spaccatura — crack
spada — sword
spago — twine, cord
spalliera — back-board

spalmare — to pitch
spargere — to spread
spassare — to unhook
spatola — putty knife
spazio — space, room
spazzare — to sweep
spazzola — brush
specchio — mirror
spedire — to send, to mail
spedizione — shipment
spegnere — to extinguish
speronare — to ram
sperone — ram, beak
spese — costs, dues
spessimetro — thickness gauge
spessore — liner, shim
spezzare — to break
spiaggia — beach
spianare — to plane, to smooth
spigolo — corner
spigone — pole
spillatura — leakage
spillo — pin
spina — eyebolt, ring bolt
spingarda — gun nozzle
spinnaco — spinnaker
spinotto — gudgeon pin
spinta — thrust
spira — coil
spiracolo — blow-hole
spiraglio — skylight
spirale — flat coil
spirare — to blow
spola — rope winch
spoletta — percussion fuse
sponderuola — rabbet plane
sporcare — to foul
sporco — foul, dirty
sportello — door
spostamento — shifting
spostare — to displace

spreco — wastage
spremere — to wring
spring — spring
spruce — spruce
spruzzare — to spray
spruzzatoio — sprinkler
spugna — sponge
spuma — spray, foam
spuntone — half spike
spurgo — drainage
squadra — square, angle iron
squadrare — to square out
squarcio — hole, rip
squilibrio — disalignment
stabile — steady, permanent
stabilimento — plant, works
stabilita — stability
staccare — to detach
staccio — sieve
stadio — stage
stagionamento — desiccation
stagnare — to tin, to solder
stagno — tin
stagnola — tin foil
stagnone — drum
staio — bushel
stalla — cattle shed
stampaggio — pressing
stampiglia — stencil
stampo — die, mould
stante — pillar
stantuffo — piston, ram
stare — to be, to stay
stazza — tonnage
stazzatura — ship tonnage
stecca — batten
stella — star
stellato — lean, wedgelike
stelo — roo, shank
stemma — ornament

stendere — to stretch out
stilo — pillar
stimare — to appraise
stiva — hold
savaggio — stowage
stoppa — oakum
stoppaccio — wad
stoppino — wick, match
storia — history
stracci — rags
strafilatura — lacing
straglio — stay
stramazzo — overfall
strangocalani — reef line
strangolare — to muzzle
strappo — jerk
strategia — strategy
strato — layer
stretto — strait, narrows
stricco — runner and tackle
stringere — to tighten
stringitoio — turning fid
striscia — strip
strizzare — to wring
stroppare — to strop, becket
strozzare — to throttle
strozzatoio — chain stopper
strozzatura — neck
strumento — instrument
struttura — framing
stucco — putty
succhiello — auger
sud — south
suggio — peg, treenail
sughero — cork
suola — sole
superficie — surface, area
supporto — rest, stand, support
svasare — to countersink
sveglia — alarm clock

svergolamento — twisting
svitare — to screw off
svolgere — to uncoil

T

tabella — table, schedule
tacca — block
tacchetto — cleat, kevel
taglia — four-sheave-block
tagliacavo — rope knife
tagliafili — wire cutter
tagliamare — cut water
tagliare — to cut
tagliatubi — pipe cutter
tagliavetro — glass cutter
tagliolo — chisel
tamburo — barrel, drum
tamponare — to stop a leak
tampone — buffer
tanaglia — cavel, kevil
tanca — tank
tappeto — pattern
tappo — plug, stopper
tarare — to calibrate
targhetta — plate, tag
tarlare — to decay
tarlato — decayed
tarlo — wood worm
tarozzo — sheer pole, rung
tassello — caulking piece
tasto — key, telegraph key
tavola — table
tavola — plank, board
tavolato — planking
tavole — tables
tazza — cup
teck — teak wood
tela — cloth, canvas
telaio — frame, rack
telefono — telephone
telegrafo — telegraph

telemetro — range finder
telescopio — telescope
tempera — hardening
temperatura — temperature
tempesta — storm
tempo — weather
tempo — time
tempra — tempering
tenaglia — nippers, pincers
tenda — awning, tent
tendaletto — boat awning
tendina — curtain
tenere — to keep, to hold
tenone — tenon
tensione — voltage
teoria — theory
termico — thermal
termometro — thermometer
termostato — thermostat
terra — land, earth
terzarolare — to reef
terzarolo — reef — (rope)
tesare — to haul up
tesascotte — cleat, kevil
tesato — taut
tessil — soft goods
tessuto — cloth
testa — head
testa a croce — crosshead
testa di moro — cap, mast cap
testiera — forward leech
tettoia — shed
tendibene — ladder hand rope
tiglio — lime
timone — rudder, helm
timoniera — wheel house
timoniera — steering compartment
timoniere — helmsman
tinozza — tub
tiraggio — draught, draft
tirante — fall, stay bar

tiranteria — linkage
tirantino — staybolt
tirare — to haul
tirastoppe — packing worm
tiro — firing shot
toccare — to touch
togliere — to remove
tondo — round
tonnellaggio — tonnage
torcere — to twist
torchio — press
torcia — torch
torelli — garboard planking
tornichetto — rigging screw
tornio — lathe
tornire — to turn on the lathe
toro — steering wheel
torpedine — torpedo, mine
torre — tower
torretta — conning-tower
torsione — twist
tracciare — to chart
tracciatura — layout
trafila — draw bench/for pipes
traguardo — sight, vang
traiettoria — trajectory
tramezzo — separating wall
tramoggia — hopper feeder
tramonto — sunset
tranciare — to sheer
trapanare — to drill, to bore
trapano — drill
trappa — hatch bar
transformare — to transform
transmissione — gear drive
trasportare — to transport
trattamento — treatment
trave — girder, beam
traversa — cross-bar
traversino — spring line
traverso — beam

travirare — to flare
travotto — studding
treccia — rope twist
trementina — turpentine
treno — train
triangolare — jib-shaped
triangolo — triangle
trinca — lashing
trincare — to lash
trincarino — stringer plate
trincatura — lashing
trinchettina — foresail
trivella — auger, borer
trivellare — to bore, to drill
tromba — ventilator cowl
trombino — steam-escape-pipe
tronco — shaft, branch
trozza — parrel, truss
trucco — traveller
truciolo — wood chip
tubazione — pipework
tubiera — boiler tubes
tubo — tube, pipe
tuffare — to dip, to douse
tuffarsi — to dive
tuga — deck house
tulipano — tulip wood
turare — to plug, to stop
turbina — turbine
turno — rotation
tuta — overalls

U

ufficio — office
ugello — nozzle
ugnare — to bevel
umidita — humidity
uncino — hook
ungere — to grease
unghia — end joint

unghietta — cross-cut chisel
unghietto — chasing-tool
unione — joint
unire — to join
unita — assembly
universo — universe
untuoso — oily
uomo — man
urtare — to collide, bump
urto — collision
uscita — exit, outlet
usura — wear
utensile — tool

V

vacante — empty
vaiolato — pitted
valore — value
valvola — valve
vampa — flash, blaze
vapore — steam
vasca — tank, basin
vascello — ship
vasi — launching ways
vassoio — tray
vedetta — lookout
vela — sail
velaccino — fore-topgallant sail
velaccio — topgallant sail
velame — sails
veliero — sailing ship
velo — veil
velocita — speed, velocity
venatura — grain (wood)
vendita — sale
venire — to come
ventilare — to fan
ventilatore — fan, blower
vento — wind
vento — guy wire
ventola — impeller

verde — green
verga bar
verghella — hoop-iron
verificare — to check; — to verify
vernice — varnish
verniciare — to paint
verricello — winch
vertice — vertex
vetro — glass
vetta — hauling line
viaggio — voyage
vibrare — to vibrate
vicino — close to
vinci — steam winch
viscosita — viscosity
visitare — to visit, to search
vista — sight
vite — screw
vitone — breech screw
voce — voice
vogare — to row, to oar
volano — flywheel
volta — turn, kink (rope)
volta — hitch, knot
voltare — to turn
volume — volume
vuoto — vacuum

Z

zaffo — boat plug
zampe di ragno — oil grooves
zattera — raft
zatterino — coper punt
zavorra — ballast
zavorrare — to ballast
zeppa — shim, wedge
zincare — to galvanize
zinco — zinc
zoccolo — pedestal
zolfo — sulphur
zona — zone, area

USEFUL TERMS

TABLE 1. ALBERI E PENNONI (MASTS AND SPARS)

1. Fuso maggiore di trinchetto — fore lower mast
2. Albero di parrochetto — fore topmast
3. Alberetto di velaccino — fore topgallant mast
4. Alberetto di controvelaccino e decontrovelaccino — fore royal and fore skysail mast
5. Fuso maggiore di maestra — main lower mast
6. Albero di gabbia — main topmast
7. Alberetto di gran velaccio — main topgallant mast
8. Alberetto di controvellaccio e decontrovelaccio — main royal and main skysail mast
9. Fuso maggiore di mezzana — mizzen lower mast
10. Albero di contromezzana — mizzen topmast
11. Alberetto di belvedere — mizzen topgallant mast
12. Alberetto di controbelvedere e decontrobelvedere — mizzen royal and mizzen skysail mast
13. Pennone maggiore di trinchetto — fore yard
14. Pennone di parrocchetto fisso — fore lower topsail yard
15. Pennone di parrochetto volante — fore upper topsail yard
16. Pennone di velaccino fisso — fore lower topgallant yard
17. Pennone di velaccino volante — fore upper topgallant yard
18. Pennone di controvelaccino — fore royal yard
19. Pennone di decontrovelaccino — fore skysail yard
20. Pennone maggiore di maestra — main yard
21. Pennone di gabbia fissa — main lower topsail yard
22. Pennone di gabbia volante — main upper topsail yard
23. Pennone di (gran) velaccio fisso — main lower topgallant yard
24. Pennone di (gran) velaccio volante — main topgallant yard
25. Pennone di controvelaccio — main royal yard
26. Pennone di decontrovelaccio — main skysail yard
27. Pennone maggiore di mezzana — crossjack yard
28. Pennone di contromezzana fissa — mizzen lower topsail yard
29. Pennone di contromezzana volante — mizzen upper topsail yard
30. Pennone di basso belvedere — mizzen lower topgallant yard

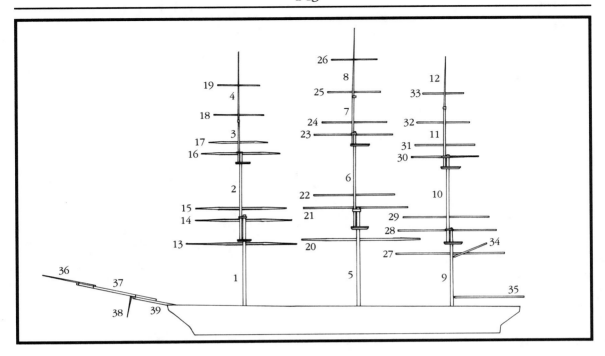

31. Pennone di belvedere volante — mizzen upper topgallant yard
32. Pennone di controbelvedere — mizzen royal yard
33. Pennone di decontrobelvedere — mizzen skysail yard
34. Picco — gaff

35. Bomma della randa (di mezzana) — gaff-sail boom
36. Asta di controfiocco — flying-jibboom
37. Asta di fiocco — jibboom
38. Pennaccino — martingale boom, dolphin striker
39. Bompresso — bowsprit

TABLE 2. MANOVRE DORMIENTI (STANDING RIGGING)

1. Straglio dell'albero di trinchetto — fore stay
2. Straglio dell'albero di parrochetto — fore topmast stay
3. Draglia del fiocco — jib stay
4. Stralletto dell'alberetto di velaccino — fore topgallant stay

5. Draglia del controfiocco — flying-jib stay
6. Stralletto dell'alberetto di controvelaccino — fore royal stay
7. Stralletto dell'alberetto di decontrovelaccino — fore skysail stay
8. Straglio dell'albero di maestra — main stay
9. Straglio dell'albero di gabbia — main topmast stay
10. Stralletto dell'alberetto di velaccio — main topgallant stay

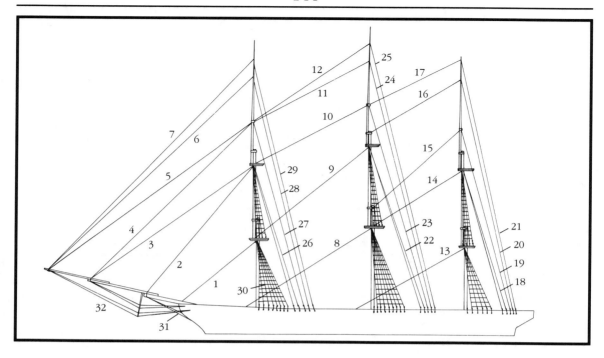

11. Stralletto dell'alberetto di controvelaccio
— main royal stay
12. Stralletto dell'alberetto di decontrovelaccio — main skysail stay
13. Straglio dell'albero di mezzana — mizzen stay
14. Straglio dell'albero di contromezzana — mizzen topmast stay
15. Stralletto dell'alberetto di belvedere — mizzen topgallant stay
16. Stralletto dell'alberetto ldi controbelvedere — mizzen royal stay
17. Stralletto dell'alberetto di decontrobelvedere — mizzen skysail stay
18. Paterazzo dell'albero di contromezzana — mizzen topmast backstay
19. Paterazzo dell'albero di belvedere — mizzen topgallant backstay
20. Paterazzetto dell'alberetto di controbelvedere — mizzen royal backstay
21. Paterazzetto dell'alberetto di decon-

trobelvedere — mizzen skysail backstay
22. Paterazzo dell'albero di gabbia — main topmast backstay
23. Paterazzo dell'albero di velaccio — main topgallant backstay
24. Paterazzetto dell'alberetto di controvelaccio — main royal backstay
25. Paterazzetto dell'alberetto di decontrovelaccio — main skysail backstay
26. Paterazzo dell'albero di parrochetto — fore topmast backstay
27. Paterazzo dell'albero di velaccino — fore topgallant backstay
28. Paterazzetto dell'alberetto di controvelaccino — fore royal backstay
29. Paterozzetto dell'alberetto di decontrovelaccino — fore skysail backstay
30. Stragli — shrouds
31. Stragli di bompresso — bowsprit shrouds (bobstays)
32. Stragli di fiocco — jibstays

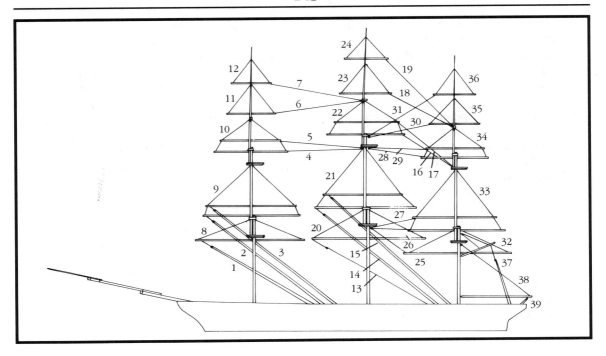

TABLE 3. MANOVRE CORRENTI (RUNNING RIGGING)

1. Braccio del pennone di trinchetto — fore brace
2. Braccio del pennone di parrochetto fisso — fore lower topsail brace
3. Braccio del pennone di parrochetto volante — fore upper topsail brace
4. Braccio del pennone di velaccino fisso — fore lower topgallant brace
5. Braccio del pennone di velaccino volante — fore upper topgallant brace
6. Braccio di controvelaccino — fore royal brce
7. Braccio di decontrovelaccino — fore skysail brace
8. Amantiglio del pennone maggiore di trinchetto — fore yard lift
9. Amantiglio del pennone di parrochetto — fore topsail yard lift
10. Amantiglio del pennone di velaccino — fore topgallant yard lift
11. Amantiglio del pennone di controvelaccino — fore royal yard lift
12. Amantiglio del pennone di decontrovelaccino — fore skysail yard lift
13. Braccio del pennone di maestra — main brace
14. Braccio del pennone di gabbia fissa — main lower topsail brace
15. Braccio del pennone di gabbia volante — main upper topsail brace
16. Braccio del pennone di velaccio fisso — main lower topgallant brace
17. Braccio del pennone di velaccio volante — main upper topgallant brace
18. Braccio del pennone di controvelaccio — main royal brace
19. Braccio del pennone di decontrovelaccio — main skysail brace

20. Amantiglio del pennone maggiore di maestra — main yard lift
21. Amantiglio del pennone di gabbia — main topmast yard lift
22. Amantiglio del pennone di velaccio — main topgallant yard lift
23. Amantiglio del pennone di controvelaccio — main royal yard lift
24. Amantiglio del pennone di decontrovelaccio — main skysail yard lift
25. Braccio del pennone di mezzana — mizzen yard brace
26. Braccio del pennone di bassa contromezzana — mizzen lower topsail brace
27. Braccio del pennone di contromezzana volante — mizzen upper topsail brace
28. Braccio del pennone di belvedere basso — mizzen lower topgallant brace
29. Braccio del pennone di belvedere volante — mizzen upper topgallant brace
30. Braccio del pennone di controbelvedere — mizzen royal yard brace
31. Braccio del pennone di decontrobelvedere — mizzen skysail yard brace
32. Amantiglio del pennone maggiore di mezzana — mizzen yard lift
33. Amantiglio del pennone di contromezzana — mizzen topmast yard lift
34. Amantiglio del pennone di belvedere — mizzen topgallant yard lift
35. Amantiglio del pennone di controbelvedere — mizzen royal yard lift
36. Amantiglio del pennone di decontrobelvedere — mizzen skysail yard lift
37. Ostino del picco — gaff vang
38. Amantiglio della randa — boom lift
39. Braccio della randa — boom brace

Glossary of useful nautical terms

aft (abaft, after) — at or toward the stern.

aloft — above the decks.

amidship (midship) — at or near the center.

athwartship — at right angles to the fore-and-aft centerline.

backing link — a strap securing the lower end of a chainplate to the hull.

back ropes — stays from the tip of the dolphin striker to each side of the bow to counter the pull of the martingale; also known as *martingale stays*.

backstay — a stay from an upper masthead leading down, out, and aft to the hull to help shrouds support the mast.

beam — a thwartship structural member on which the deck is laid; the width dimension of a hull.

becket — the rope or metal eye at the bottom of a block through which the standing part of a purchase is made fast.

bee seat — a fairlead on the side of the bowsprit (generally starboard) near its outer end through which are lead the upper stays.

belay — to make fast a rope; to stop.

belaying pin — a stout wood or iron pin set in a socket around which lines are secured—like a cleat.

belfry — a support for the ship's bell.

bend (bend on) — to fasten in place, as in *bending sail.*

bentinck shroud — an arrangement to secure futtock shrouds against the pull of the topmast in which shrouds are crossed as they are led to a purchase on deck.

bibbs — large wood plates on the sides of masts that support the trestletrees; sometimes called *cheek knees.*

billboard — a slanting platform at the ship's side, abaft the catheads, on which the flukes of old-fashioned anchors rested when stowed.

binnacle — the compass housing.

bitts — heavy iron or wood posts (single or in pairs) around which ropes are belayed; single ones are generally called bollards.

block — a pulley; one sheave—*single block*; two sheaves—*double block*, etc.

boat deck — the uppermost deck on which lifeboats are stowed.

bobstay — a stay from the bowsprit tip to the stem near the cutwater.

bolster — a rounded piece of wood to prevent chafing of rigging.

boom — the spar at the foot of a fore-and-aft sail.

braces — ropes used to swing the yards and control their position.

breeching — a heavy rope to take the recoil of carriage guns.

bridge mast — sometimes called *pair masts*; similar to kingposts but with heads connected by a truss or bridge-like structure.

bulkhead — any vertical partition separating compartments.

bulwark — a closed or solid rail along the ship's side.

bumpkin — a strut projecting from the hull to take certain running rigging.

cap — a block that joins the end of one spar to another—as in *mastcap* or *bowsprit cap.*

caprail — a flat covering piece on the top of a rail or bulwark.

capstan — an upright wood or metal cylinder mounted on deck that was used to haul the anchor or to get a strong pull on a line.

carrick bitts — the upright timbers to which is fastened the wooden barrel windlass.

cathead — a timber projecting over each bow; see also *fish tackle.*

cavil (cavel) — a long wooden cleat for belaying larger lines.

chainplate — chain or an iron rod to secure the lower deadeye to the hull.

chain pipe — vertical pipes abaft the windlass leading to the chain locker; also called *naval pipes.*

channel — a wooden platform projecting from the hull over which the chainplates lie; originally *chain wales.*

charlie noble — the galley smoke pipe or chimney.

chock — a fairlead fitting in a bulwark or rail for passage of a hawser—circular ones are *mooring pipes*; also a support to hold a boat or other stowed gear off the deck.

cleat — a fitting with two horns on which a rope is belayed.

clew — the lower corners of a square sail and the lower after corner of a fore-and-aft sail.

coaming — vertical construction similar to bulwarks around deck openings such as hatches and cockpits.

companionway — the stairways in a ship.

counter — the overhang of a vessel's stern.

course — the lowest and largest square sail on a mast—*forecourse, maincourse*, etc.

crane — the support outside the ship's hull on which a small boat rests; also, the fitting (sometimes called a cranse iron) to hold a lower topsail yard to the lower mastcap.

crossjack (pronounced *crossjik*) — the lower yard on the mizzenmast; American shipmasters were the first to set a sail from this yard.

crosstrees — thwartship timbers resting on the trestletrees that spread the topmast shrouds.

cutwater — that part of the stem above the waterline.

davit — metal or wood derricks of various construction to hoist boats, anchors, supplies, etc.

deadeye — a round wood block with three holes; used to set up standing rigging.

devil's claw — a fork and turnbuckle arrangement put on the anchor chain to retain the anchor in the hawse pipe at sea.

dolphin striker — a spar or rod extending down from the bowsprit cap.

doubling — the overlapping section of upper and lower mast between trestletrees and cap.

draft — the distance in feet and inches from the surface of the water to the bottom of the keel.

entrance — the forward part of the hull below the waterline.

eyebrow — a small metal piece fastened above a port to keep out rain drippings; also called a *wriggle*.

fairlead — a metal or wooden ring or loop that guides a rope in the required direction.

fairwater — additional material built around an underwater projection from the hull to smooth the flow of water.

fid — a large wooden pin in the heel of a topmast.

fiferail — a rail around a mast to hold belaying pins—similar to a pinrail.

figurehead — a carved image on a ship's stem.

fish tackle — a three-fold purchase rigged at the cathead to raise the anchor from the water to the billboard; the rope of this purchase is the *catfall*.

Flemish horse — a short footrope at the extremity of a yard.

footrope — a rope hanging on the after side of a yard on which sailors stand.

fore (forward) — toward or near the bow.

forecastle (pronounced *fawksil*) — the raised section of the deck at the bow; also, the crew's quarters.

forefoot — the point where the stem meets the keel.

foremast — the mast nearest the bow.

frame — a thwartship structural member of the hull (a rib).

futtock band — a metal band around the mast below the bibbs to which are fastened the futtock shrouds.

futtock shrouds — short iron rods from the futtock band to the ends of the crosstrees that secure the lower ends of the topmast shrouds.

futtock stave — a short, leather-covered iron or wood rod lashed where the futtocks cross the shrouds as a fairlead for the running rigging; originally the futtocks were lashed to it.

gaff — a spar to extend and hold the head of a fore-and-aft sail.

galley — the kitchen; also, a type of Mediterranean vessel propelled by oars and sails.

gallow frame (pronounced *gallis*) — a light framework above the deck on which boats and extra gear are stowed.

gammoning — the fastening at the stemhead to hold down the bowsprit; originally rope, it evolved into an iron strap.

gangway — the opening in the bulwarks for entering or leaving a vessel; the accommodation ladder rigged at the gangway is often so-called.

gooseneck — a type of universal joint at the heel of a boom.

gudgeon — the metal socket on the sternpost in which the rudder pintle fits and turns.

gunport — an opening in the hull or bulwark through which the guns are fired.

guy — a line or purchase used to steady a boom.

gypsy head — a small drum with filleted flanges at each end to better handle line.

halyard (halliard) — the rope or purchase used to hoist sails or yards — originally *haul yard*.

hatch — the cover for an opening in the deck

harness cask — a barrel used to keep meat in brine; the meat is called *salt horse*.

hawse pipe — the pipe at the bow through which the anchor cable passes.

hawser — a heavy rope for tying a vessel to a pier, towing, etc.

hawser reel — a drum on which heavy lines and wires are wound for stowage.

head — the upper side of a square sail; the upper side of a triangular fore-and-aft sail; the upper end of a mast, etc.

heel — the lower end of a mast; the inboard end of a bowsprit, etc.; the tilt of a vessel due to wave or wind action.

hounds — the flattened sides of a mast near the head to which are fastened the bibbs.

jackstay — the small iron rods on top of a yard to which sails are fastened; also, the fixed wire on stanchions to which an awning is lashed.

jaw — as gaff or boom—wooden horns fastened to each side of the heel of a spar to hold it in line with the mast.

jib — a triangular sail set on a stay ahead of the foremast.

jibboom — the extension of a bowsprit—similar to a topmast on a lower mast.

keel — the main fore-and-aft structural member (backbone) of a hull, to which are fastened the stem, sternpost, and frames.

kingpost — a short, stout mast near the side of a cargo vessel for supporting a cargo boom.

knighthead — vertical posts near the bow that support and confine the bowsprit heel.

lanyard — a short, light rope—used as a lashing, for example to attach shrouds or stays, through deadeyes, to the hull.

leech — the side edges of a square sail and the after edge of a fore-and-aft sail.

lubber's hole — the opening in a masttop platform for shrouds and running rigging. A true sailor would *never* climb through the lubber's hole when going aloft.

luff — the forward edge of a fore-and-aft sail; to head the sail directly into the wind.

mainmast — the primary and largest mast on a vessel.

martingale — a stay from the end of the jibboom to the tip of the dolphin striker.

masthead — the section from the eyes of the rigging to the masttop.

mast wedges — blocks shaped and tapered to fit around a mast at the deck to hold it firmly in place.

mizzenmast — the mast next aft of the mainmast.

monkey rail — a short pinrail near the bow on which to belay the jib and staysail downhauls.

parrel — a rope, wood, or iron collar that secures a yard to a mast.

peak — outboard end of a gaff or that corner of the sail attached thereto; the spaces in the ends of a hull.

pendant — a short rope or wire to which a block is fastened.

pitch — the angle a mast leans forward of the vertical.

pinrail — a horizontal timber along the bulwarks with holes to receive belaying pins.

pintle — pins or bolts on the forward edge of a rudder that fit into the gudgeon, allowing the rudder to pivot.

plimsoll mark — a mark on the side of the hull about midship, port and starboard, to show the maximum draft allowed by law; originated by Samuel Plimsoll in the British Parliament in 1876.

pole — the topmost section of the uppermost mast; a vessel is *pole masted* if its masts are not fitted for topmasts; a vessel is *baldheaded* if it is fitted for topmasts, but the masts are not stepped.

poop — the raised deck at the after end of a merchant vessel—similar to the quarter deck of a naval vessel.

port — the left side of a ship when facing forward; originally, and in some inland waters, called *larboard*; also, an opening in the side of a hull or deckhouse.

purchase — a tackle that increases the force applied through an arrangement of pulleys.

P/S — on a plan, a designation that the item shown is on both the port and starboard sides.

quarter — the portion of a ship between midship and the stern, and things attached thereto, as in *quarter boat, quarter galley*.

quoin — a bevelled block under the breech of a gun to change it elevation; any angular chock to support and wedge casks or other round objects stowed in a ship's hold.

rabbet line — the line where the outside of the hull material (planking or plating) meets the stem, keel, and sternpost.

rake — the angle a mast leans aft of the vertical.

ratline — small ropes fastened across the shrouds to form a ladder for going aloft.

reeve — to run a rope through a hole or block; to assemble a purchase.

ring stopper — the rope or chain holding the upper end of an anchor to the billboard.

robband — a small piece of line to fasten the head of a sail to its yard— originally *rope bands*.

royal mast — the section of the topgallant mast above the topgallant rigging.

rubbing strake — a timber on the outside of the hull at or near the sheer line to protect the hull; also called the *guard rail* or *rubbing strip*.

run — the underwater, after part of the hull—where it *runs away* from the water.

running rigging — ropes and blocks used to set and control the spars and sails.

saddle — a block on the after side of a yard shaped to fit a mast.

samson post — a short, stout timber projecting above the deck to which a derrick is rigged for hoisting cargo, or a mooring line is made fast.

scupper — a hole in the bulwark to carry off water from the deck.

scuttle — a small hatchway and its cover; to intentionally sink a ship by opening its seacock or cutting holes in the ship's bottom or sides.

shank painter — the rope or chain securing the fluke of an anchor to the billboard.

sheave (pronounced *shiv*) — a grooved wheel in a block.

sheer — the curve of the deck from bow to stern; *take a sheer* is to suddenly change course.

sheet — the rope fastened to the clew of a sail.

ship — technically a three- or more masted vessel, square rigged on all masts; generally, any large vessel. (An old rhyme will help : *A vessel is something on the ocean that floats, the big ones are ships, the little ones boats.*

shroud — part of the standing rigging; rope or wire from a masthead to the hull sides to support the masts athwartship.

skylight — a deck structure with openings to allow light and air into the hull or cabins.

skysail — the small square sail set above a royal.

sling — a rope or chain strap used to secure the center section of a yard to the mast.

spanker — the fore-and-aft sail on the after mast.

spar — a general term for yards, masts, booms, gaffs, and bowsprits; a piece of round timber.

spencer mast — a small diameter spar immediately aft of and attached at head and heel to the lower mast; the sail set there on the mainmast is the spencer.

spring stay — a horizontal stay between two mastheads.

spreader — a strutlike spar similar to a crosstree.

stanchion — a small vertical rod or timber to support a rail; in wooden ships, a rough log used as a pillar in the ship's hold.

standing rigging — all fixed rigging, such as shrouds and stays.

starboard — the right side of a vessel when facing forward.

stay — a fixed rope to support a mast in a fore-and-aft direction.

stem — the upright post at the bow to which the ends of the side planks are fastened.

stern — the after end of the ship.

sternpost — the vertical timber at the after end of the hull.

steeve — the angle of the bowsprit above the horizontal.

stirrup — short ropes from the jackstay of a yard to support the footropes.

strake — one row of plating or planking that forms the skin of the hull; *garboard strake* is the row next to the keel; *bilge strake* is the row at the turn of the bilge; *sheer strake* is the row at the top of the hull side.

tack — the lower forward corner of a fore-and-aft sail; the rope that holds down the forward clew of a square sail when *on the wind*; to change the vessel's relation to the wind, as in *we tacked to port*.

tackle — a combination of rope and blocks; a purchase.

taffrail — the rail around the stern of a vessel.

throat — the forward upper corner of a fore-and-aft sail.

thwart — the seat in a small boat.

tiller — a bar to turn the rudder; also called the *helm*.

timber head — that part of the wooden frames that project above the deck on which the bulwarks are built.

toggle — a wooden pin with a short piece of rope fastened to its center; the eye in the other end of the rope is the *salamander*.

top — a platform built on the crosstrees.

topgallant — the mast above the topmast; the sail set from the yard *gansil*.

topping lift — a rope or purchase to hold up and control the horizontal angle of a yard or boom.

trail board — a decorative piece extending from the stemhead to the bow; also called the *headboard*.

train tackle — the purchase to haul a gun inboard for cleaning and reloading.

transom — the flat, upright part of a vessel's stern.

triatic stay — a wire stay on a fore-and-aft rigged vessel leading from the topmast head to the lower masthead of the mast immediately aft.

traveler — an iron ring, thimble, or snap that *travels* on a spar, rope, or bar.

trestletree — fore-and-aft timbers resting on the bibbs at the masthead.

truck — the capping piece at the top a mast; also, the wheel of a carriage gun.

truss — the iron fittings holding a lower yard to the mast.

tryworks — the stove rig on a whaler's deck to boil the oil out of blubber.

tumblehome — the slope inward of a hull side from the waterline to the deck.

tye (tie) — the part of the purchase for hoisting a yard that passes through a sheave mounted in the mast.

vang — a purchase with a pendant leading from the peak of a gaff.

wale — an extra heavy strake of planking that strengthens the side at certain places, such as the gunwale (pronounced *gunnel*).

waterway — a channel next to the bulwark to lead deck water to the scuppers.

whisker boom — a spar projecting port and starboard from the bowsprit cap to spread the jibboom stays.

wildcat — the grooved wooden wheel on a windlass over which the anchor chain passes.

windlass — a ratcheted winch used to hoist and weigh anchors.

woolding — bands of metal or turns of rope around a lower mast to strengthen it, as in large diameter wood masts.

yard — an athwartship spar from which a square sail is set; or a small spar from which signals are flown, a *signal yard*.

yoke — part of the fittings of a lower yard used with a truss.

Suggested reading list

Some of these classics are out of print and may be difficult to find at your neighborhood bookstore. Try libraries, hobby shops, secondhand booksellers—the effort will be worth it.

Campbell, George F. *China Tea Clippers*. Camden, Maine: International Marine Publishing Company, 1990. (Originally published in Great Britain by Adlard Coles Ltd., 1974.)

Chapelle, Howard I. *The History of American Sailing Ships*. New York: W. W. Norton & Company, 1935.

Chapelle, Howard I. *The Search for Speed Under Sail 1700-1855*. New York: W. W. Norton & Company, 1967.

Lees, James. *The Masting and Rigging of English Ships of War 1624-1860*. Annapolis, Md.: Naval Institute Press, 1979.

Lever, Darcy. *The Young Sea Officer's Sheet Anchor*. New York: Edward W. Sweetman Co., 1963.

Underhill, Harold A. *Masting & Rigging the Clipper Ship & Ocean Carrier*. Glasgow: Brown, Son & Ferguson, 1988.

INDEX